PowerPoint 97 for Windows Made Simple

Moira Stephen

MADE SIMPLE
BOOKS

Made Simple
An imprint of Butterworth-Heinemann
Linacre House, Jordan Hill, Oxford OX2 8DP
225 Wildwood Avenue, Woburn, MA 01801-2041
A division of Reed Educational and Professional Publishing Ltd

A member of the Reed Elsevier plc group

OXFORD   BOSTON   JOHANNESBURG
MELBOURNE   NEW DELHI   SINGAPORE

First published 1997
Reprinted 1998

British Library Cataloguing in Publication Data
A catalogue record for this book is available from the British Library

ISBN 07506 3799 4

 Typeset by P.K.McBride, Southampton

Archtype, Bash Casual, Cotswold and Gravity fonts from Advanced Graphics Ltd
Icons designed by Sarah Ward © 1994
Printed and bound in Great Britain by Scotprint, Musselburgh, Scotland

COMPUTING
MADE SIMPLE

This is the best liked and most user friendly series of Computer books for PC users.

The original and the best.

These books explain the basics of software packages and computer topics in a clear and simple manner, providing just enough information to get started. They are ideal for users who want an insight into software packages and computers without being overwhelmed by technical terminology.

ALL YOU NEED TO GET STARTED

- **Easy to Follow**
- **Task Based**
- **Jargon Free**
- **Easy Steps**
- **Practical**
- **Excellent Value**

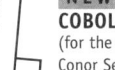

Contents

Preface

The computer is about as simple as a spacecraft, and whoever let an untrained spaceman loose? You pick up a manual that weighs more than your birth-weight, open it and find that its written in computerspeak. You see messages on the screen that look like code and the thing even makes noises. No wonder that you feel it's your lucky day if everything goes right. What do you do if everything goes wrong? Give up.

Training helps. Being able to type helps. Experience helps. This book helps, by providing training and assisting with experience. It can't help you if you always manage to hit the wrong keys, but it can tell you which are the right ones and what to do when you hit the wrong ones. After some time, even the dreaded manual will start to make sense, just because you know what the writers are wittering on about.

Computing is not black magic. You don't need luck or charms, just a bit of understanding. The problem is that the programs that are used nowadays look simple but aren't. Most of them are crammed with features you don't need – but how do you know what you don't need? This book shows you what is essential and guides you through it. You will know how to make an action work and why. The less essential bits can wait – and once you start to use a program with confidence you can tackle these bits for yourself.

The writers of this series have all been through it. We know your time is valuable, and you don't want to waste it. You don't buy books on computer subjects to read jokes or be told that you are a dummy. You want to find what you need and be shown how to achieve it. Here, at last, you can.

1 Getting Started

What is PowerPoint?

PowerPoint 97 for Windows is a presentation graphics package. If you have to make presentations, PowerPoint gives you the tools you need to produce your own materials with little or no help from presentation graphics specialists.

You can use PowerPoint to produce:

Slides

Slides are the individual pages of your presentation. They may contain text, graphs, clip art, tables, drawings, animation, video clips, visuals created in other applications, shapes – and more!! PowerPoint will allow you to run your slide show on your computer, or as 35mm slides or overhead projector transparencies.

Speaker's notes (Chapters 5, 9 and 11)

A speaker's notes page accompanies each slide you create. Each notes page contains a small image of the slide plus any notes you type in. You can print the pages and use them to prompt you during your presentation.

Handouts (Chapters 9 and 11)

Handouts consist of smaller, printed versions of your slides which can be printed 2, 3 or 6 slides to a page. They provide useful backup material for your audience and can be customised with your company name or logo.

Outline (Chapters 4 and 11)

A presentation Outline contains the slide titles and main text items, but neither art nor text typed in using the text tool. The Outline gives a useful overview of your presentation's structure.

Take note

A PowerPoint presentation is a collections of slides, with optional, but useful support materials, notes, handouts and an outline, all in one file.

Basic steps

Getting into PowerPoint

1 Click the **Start** button on the Taskbar.

2 Select **Programs**.

3 Choose **PowerPoint**.

Is PowerPoint installed on your computer? If it isn't, install it now (or get someone else to do it for you).

If necessary, switch on your computer and go into Windows. You are now ready to start.

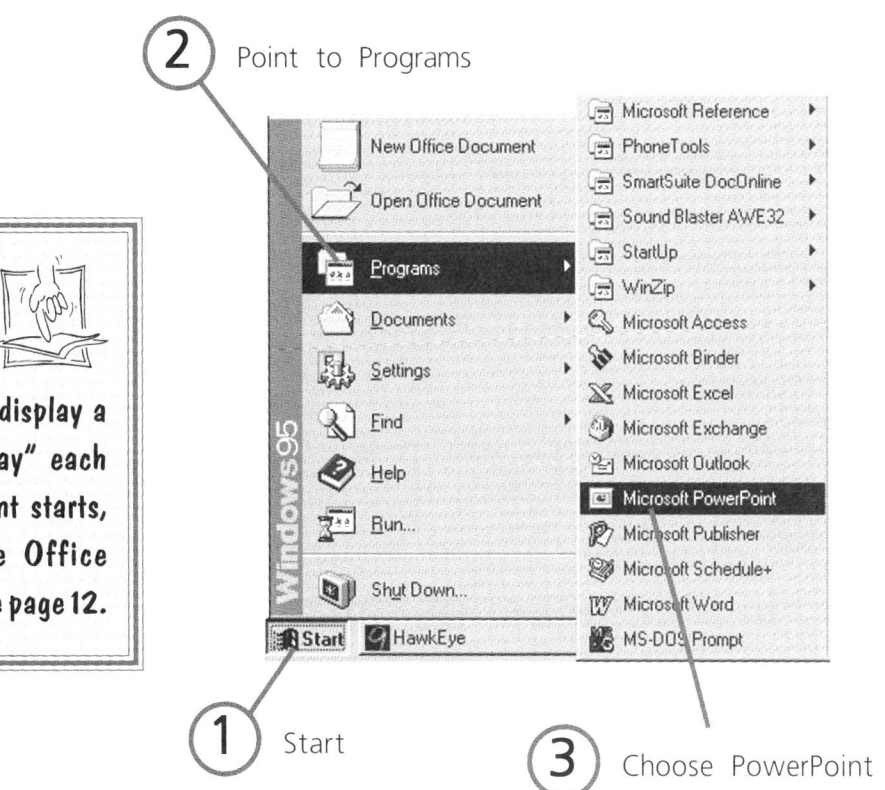

Take note

If you want to display a "Tip of the Day" each time PowerPoint starts, customise the Office Assistant — see page 12.

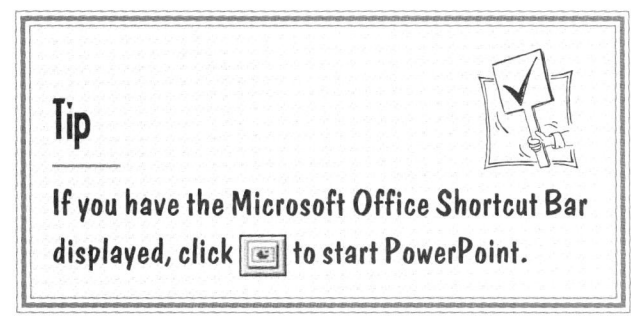

Tip

If you have the Microsoft Office Shortcut Bar displayed, click ▣ to start PowerPoint.

PowerPoint dialog box

You arrive at the PowerPoint dialog box, where you start to set up your presentation.

AutoContent wizard

Choose this if you want to start by using a Wizard that helps you work out the content and organisation of your presentation.

Template

This option lets you pick a presentation template with the colour scheme, fonts and other design features already set up.

Blank presentation

If you opt for this one, you get a blank presentation with all the colour scheme, font and design features set to the default values.

Tip

If you need to know more about Windows 95, try the companion volume in this series – *Windows 95 Made Simple.*

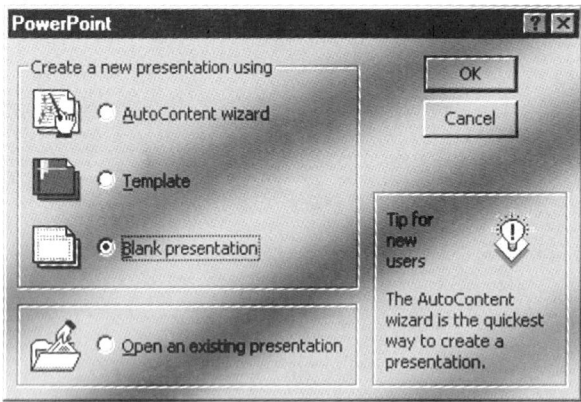

Open an existing presentation

This option takes you to the Open dialog box, where you can open an existing presentation.

PowerPoint window

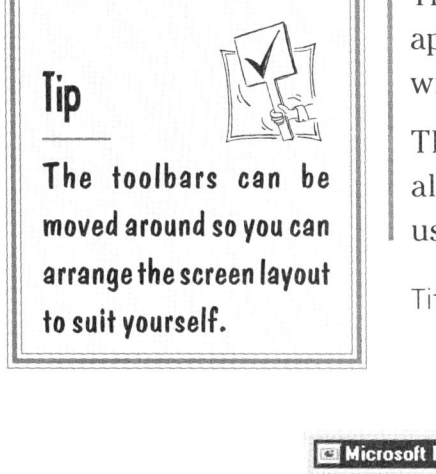

Tip

The toolbars can be moved around so you can arrange the screen layout to suit yourself.

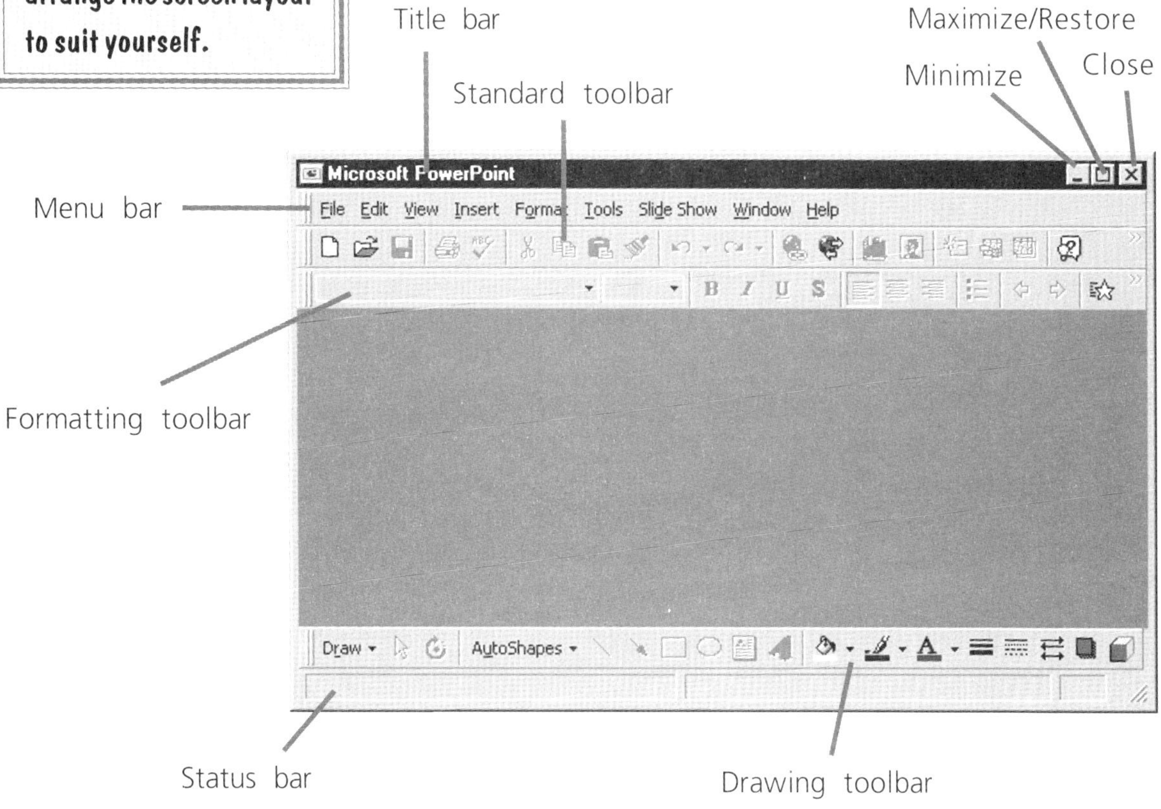

The PowerPoint window is very similar to other Microsoft application windows. If you use Word, Excel or Access you will recognise some of the tools on the toolbars.

The Standard and Formatting toolbars usually appear along the top of the window. The Drawing toolbar is usually along the bottom of the window.

Title bar

Maximize/Restore

Minimize   Close

Standard toolbar

Menu bar

Microsoft PowerPoint

File Edit View Insert Format Tools Slide Show Window Help

B I U S

Formatting toolbar

Draw ▾   AutoShapes ▾

Status bar

Drawing toolbar

Leaving PowerPoint

Leaving PowerPoint is very easy. If you use other Windows packages, the technique is very similar. Just click on the Close button or open the **File** menu and choose **Exit.**

PowerPoint objects

When working in PowerPoint you work with *objects*. The objects may be:

- Text
- Drawings
- Graphs
- Organisation charts
- Clip art
- Movies
- Sounds
- Tables

Take note

You'll learn how to create and manipulate these objects as you work with the package.

Sea Creatures

- Butterflyfish
- Spotted Triggerfish
- Surgeonfish
- Squid
- Garibaldi
- Stingray

Clip art can enliven your text – a wide variety of images are supplied with PowerPoint

Annotated graphs can be produced very easily

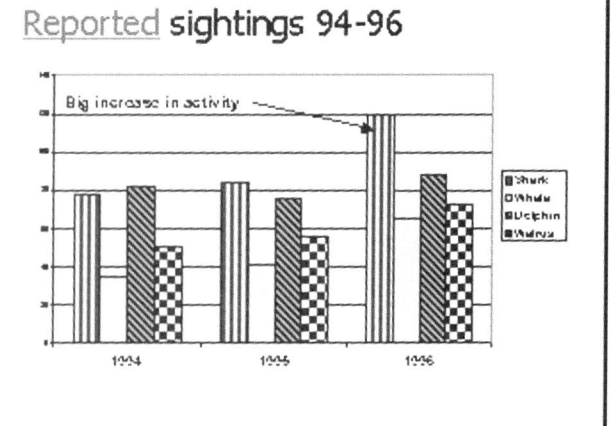

Reported sightings 94-96

6

There are several movies and sounds supplied with PowerPoint

Organisation charts are simple to create – once you've worked out the structure of your organisation!

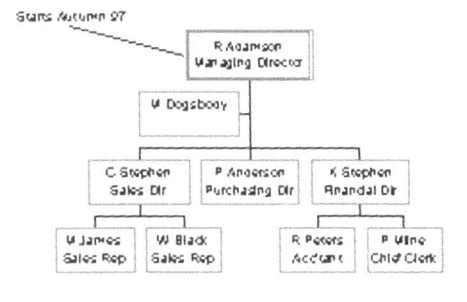

New Appointment Structure

Starts Autumn 97

R Adamson
Managing Director

W Dogsbody

C Stephen
Sales Dir

P Anderson
Purchasing Dir

K Stephen
Financial Dir

W James
Sales Rep

W Black
Sales Rep

R Peters
Accountant

P Milne
Chief Clerk

Visitors to Education Centre

	Adult	Child	Member	Total
Jan	402	675	300	1377
Feb	542	865	430	1837
Mar	499	621	523	1643
Apr	1845	2300	1954	6099
Total	3288	4461	3207	10956

Word tables are useful for displaying statistics

Summary

❑ PowerPoint is a powerful **presentation graphics** package.

❑ The **PowerPoint dialog box** gives you a range of options to get you started creating your presentation.

❑ The PowerPoint window displays a selection of **toolbars** to give you quick access to commonly used features in the package.

❑ Text, drawings, graphs, Organisation charts, clip art, movies, sounds and tables are called PowerPoint **Objects.**

❑ To exit PowerPoint, click the Close button on the title bar.

2 Help

Office Assistant

When working in the Windows environment there is always plenty of help available – in books, in manuals, in magazines and on-line. The trick is being able to find the help you need, when you need it. In this section, we look at the various ways you can interrogate the on-line Help when you discover you're in need of it.

One of the first things you'll notice when working with any of the Office 97 applications is the 'Office Assistant'. This new interface to the on-line help system is unique and replaces the Answer Wizard found in Office 95. The Office Assistant displays help topics and tips to help you accomplish your tasks. It interacts with you through its 'dialog bubble', rather than a standard dialog box!

Basic steps

1 To display the Office Assistant press [F1].

or

Click [?].

2 Click an item in the list for Help on that topic.

or

3 Type in your question and click (● **Search**).

4 The Help topic(s) will appear on your screen.

5 To close Help, click the Close ☒ button at the top right of its window.

6 To close the Assistant, click ☒ on its title bar.

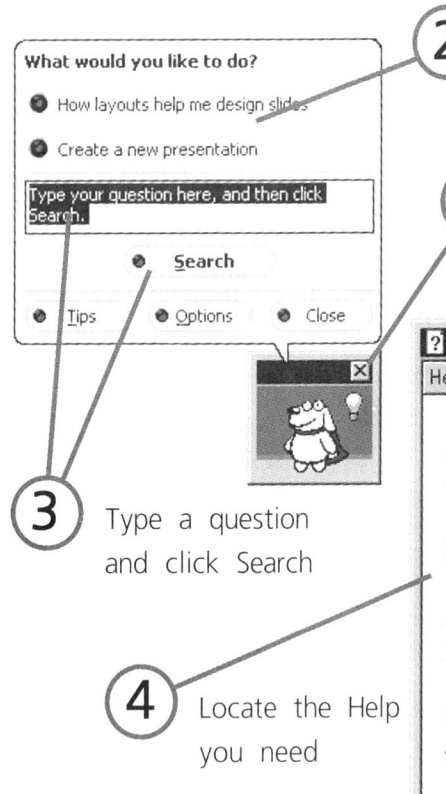

② Choose an item

⑥ Close the Assistant

③ Type a question and click Search

④ Locate the Help you need

⑤ Close the page

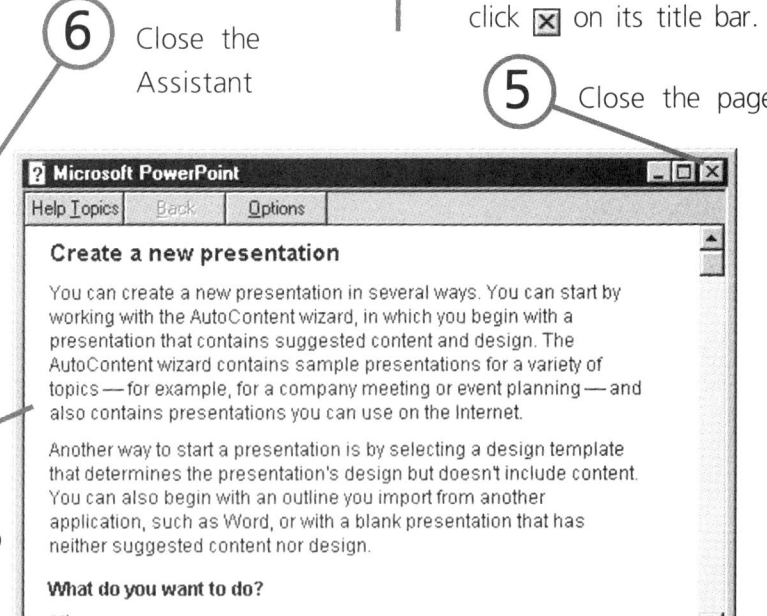

Basic steps

1 If you have closed the Office Assistant, display it – click 🔲.

2 Click the Tips button (● Tips). The Office Assistant will display its 'Tip of the day'.

3 Click (● Next) to display the next tip, or (● Back) to go back to the previous tip. (If either option is dimmed, you are either at the beginning or the end of the list of tips.)

4 When you've finished viewing the tips, click (● Close).

You may keep the Office Assistant open while you work – you can drag it (using the title bar on the Office Assistant) to a suitable area of the screen (one that doesn't obscure what you are working on) and leave it there.

To display its list of Help options (which vary depending on what you are doing), or to type in a question, simply give it a click!

Big Brother is watching you!

The Office Assistant is constantly monitoring your actions. If you perform an action for which there is a useful shortcut, or a quick alternative method of doing, the Office Assistant lights up to indicate that it has a tip that you may find useful.

Click the light bulb to display the tip.

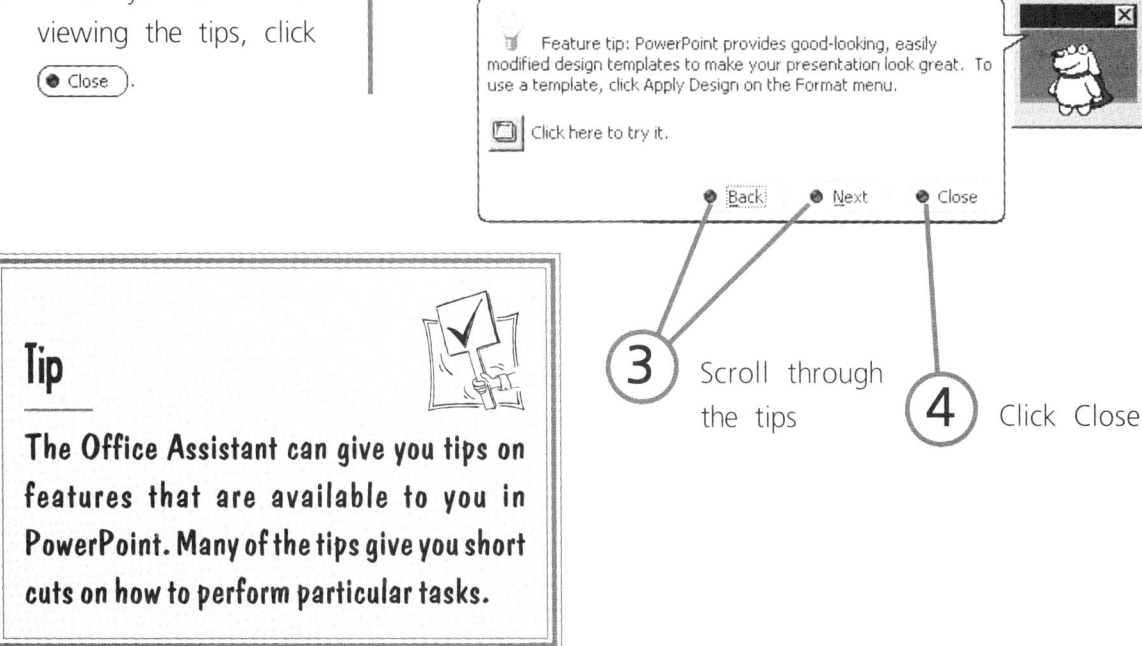

③ Scroll through the tips

④ Click Close

Tip

The Office Assistant can give you tips on features that are available to you in PowerPoint. Many of the tips give you short cuts on how to perform particular tasks.

Customising the Office Assistant

You can customise the Office Assistant to take on a different appearance or to behave in the way you find most useful.

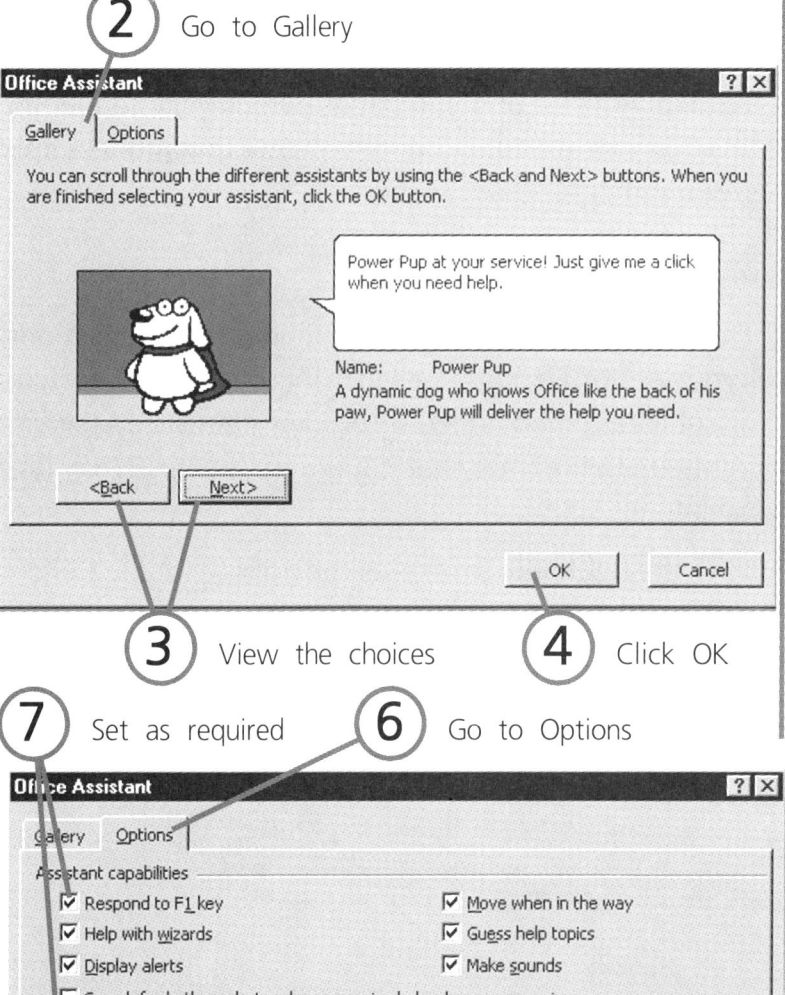

② Go to Gallery

③ View the choices ④ Click OK

⑦ Set as required ⑥ Go to Options

❏ **Appearance**

1 Click (⊙ Options) in the Assistant's bubble.

2 Select the **Gallery** tab.

3 Use [Next>] and [<Back] to see the personalities.

4 Click [OK] when you find the one that you want to use.

❏ **Other options**

5 Click (⊙ Options) in the ASsistant's bubble.

6 Select the **Options** tab.

7 Select or deselect the options as required.

8 Click [OK].

Take note

If you leave the Assistant open while you work, (⊙ Options) is dimmed in some dialog boxes, e.g. **Open**.

⑧ Click OK

Basic steps

1 Hold down the [Shift] key and press [F1].

The mouse pointer looks like this ▶?.

❏ **To find out what a particular tool does**

2 Click the tool.

or

❏ **To find out about an item in a menu list**

3 Open the menu list by clicking on the menu name.

4 Click on the option required on the menu.

or

❏ **To find out about anything else within the application window**

5 Just click on it.

Take note

You must have a presentation open to enable the What's This feature.

What's This?

If you are new to Microsoft Office applications or to the Windows interface, there will be many things on your screen that puzzle you at first.

There may be strange looking tools on the toolbars; items listed in the menus may suggest things you've never heard of and other objects that appear and disappear as you work may add to your confusion!

Don't panic! If you don't know what it is – ask!

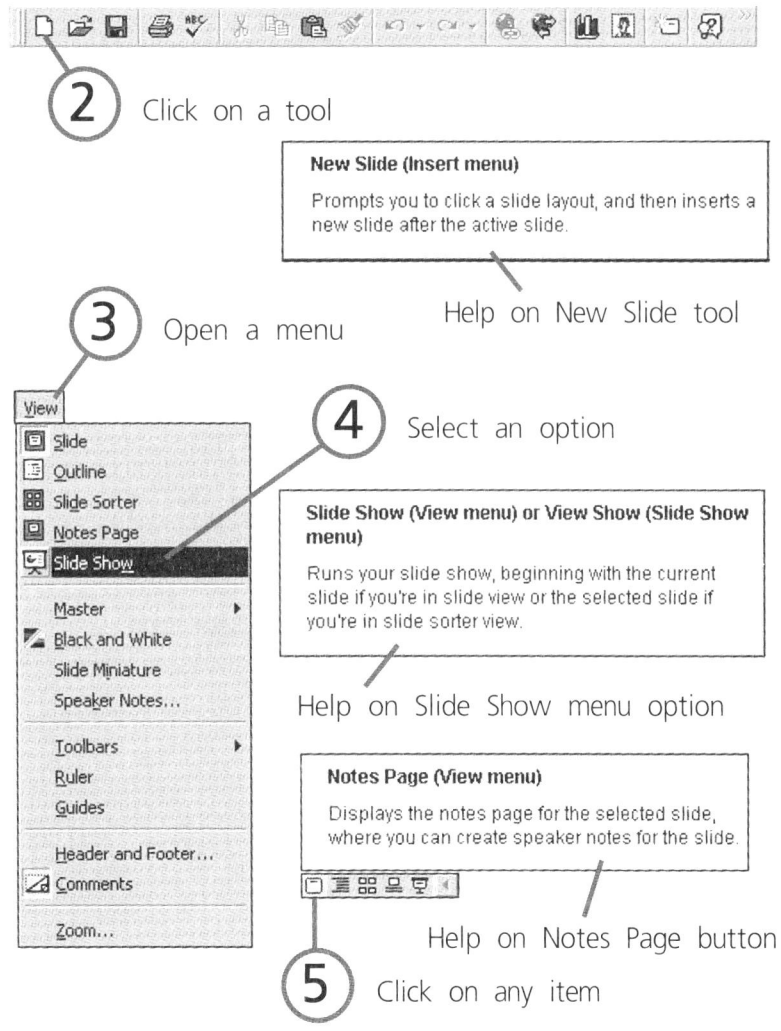

② Click on a tool

New Slide (Insert menu)
Prompts you to click a slide layout, and then inserts a new slide after the active slide.

Help on New Slide tool

③ Open a menu

④ Select an option

Slide Show (View menu) or View Show (Slide Show menu)
Runs your slide show, beginning with the current slide if you're in slide view or the selected slide if you're in slide sorter view.

Help on Slide Show menu option

Notes Page (View menu)
Displays the notes page for the selected slide, where you can create speaker notes for the slide.

Help on Notes Page button

⑤ Click on any item

ScreenTips

If you point to any tool on a displayed toolbar, a ScreenTip appears to describe the function of the tool.

If you like using keyboard shortcuts, you can customise the ScreenTips to display the shortcut as well. This will help you learn the shortcuts quickly.

You can have large icons if they will help

③ Go to Options

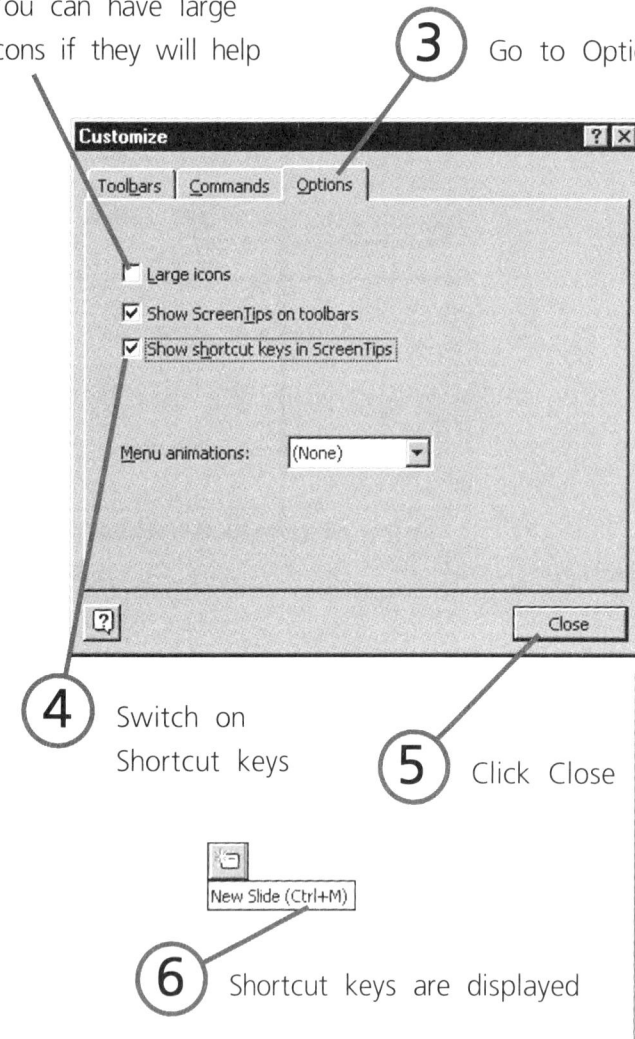

④ Switch on Shortcut keys

⑤ Click Close

⑥ Shortcut keys are displayed

- ❏ To customise the ScreenTips
- **1** Point to any toolbar that is displayed and click the right mouse button.
- **2** Choose **Customize...** from the shortcut menu.
- **3** Select the **Options** tab in the **Customize** dialog box.
- **4** Select the **Show shortcut keys** in ScreenTips option.
- **5** Click **Close**.
- **6** Point to a tool on the toolbar – if it has a shortcut key it will be displayed with the screen tip.

Take note

If you've used previous versions of PowerPoint, take a look through **What's New in PowerPoint** on the Contents tab in the on-line **Help**.

Basic steps

1 Open the **Help** menu and choose **Contents and Index**.

2 At the **Help Topics** dialog box, select the **Contents** tab.

3 Select a book and click [_Open_] or double-click on it. You may see more books, a list of topics, or both. Open the books as needed.

4 To open a topic, select it and click [_Display_] or double-click.

5 Work through the Help system until you find the Help you need.

6 Close the Help system.

The Help system can also be accessed through the Help menu. Almost everything you'll ever need to know will be somewhere in these Help pages. The Help pages can be located from the Contents, Index or Find tabs.

Contents tab

The Contents tab is a good place to 'browse'. Look through the topics and explore any that appeal to you.

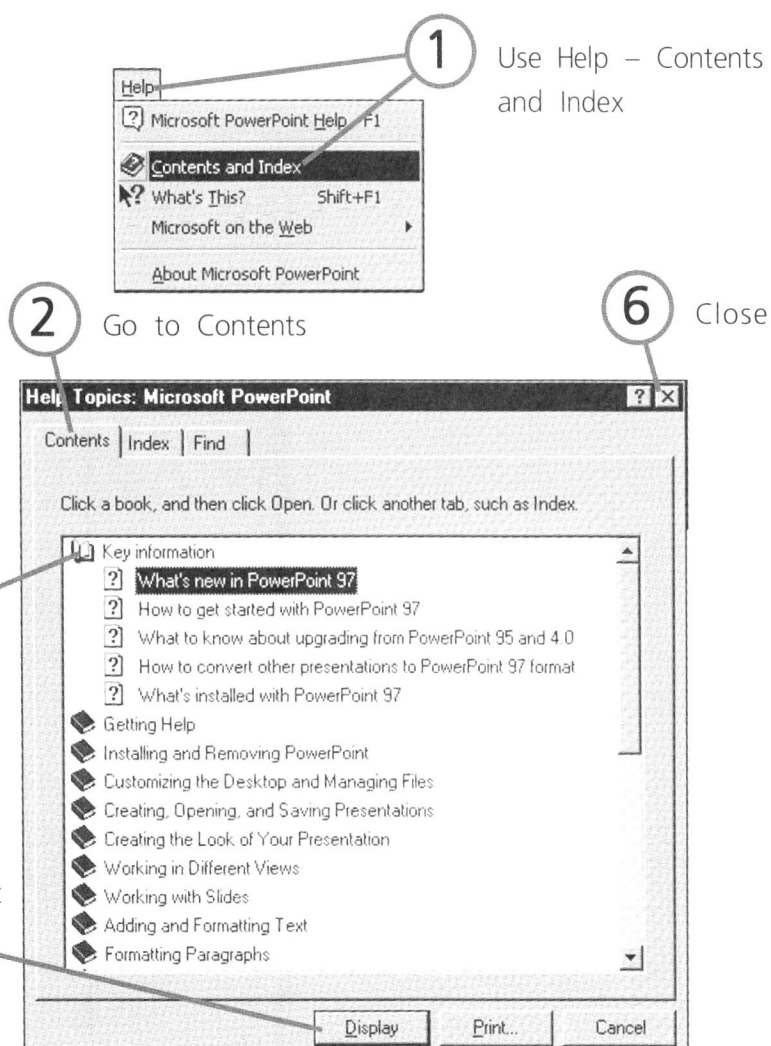

1 Use Help – Contents and Index

2 Go to Contents

6 Close

3 Open a book

4 Display a topic

This shows **Open** or **Close** when you select a book

Index tab

The Index tab gives you quick access to any topic and is particularly useful if you know what you are looking for!

1 Select the **Index** tab.

2 Start typing the word you're looking for.

3 Select an index entry from the list.

4 Click ⬚ Display ⬚. You will see a list of topics or a Help page.

5 Continue until you find the Help you need.

6 Close the Help system.

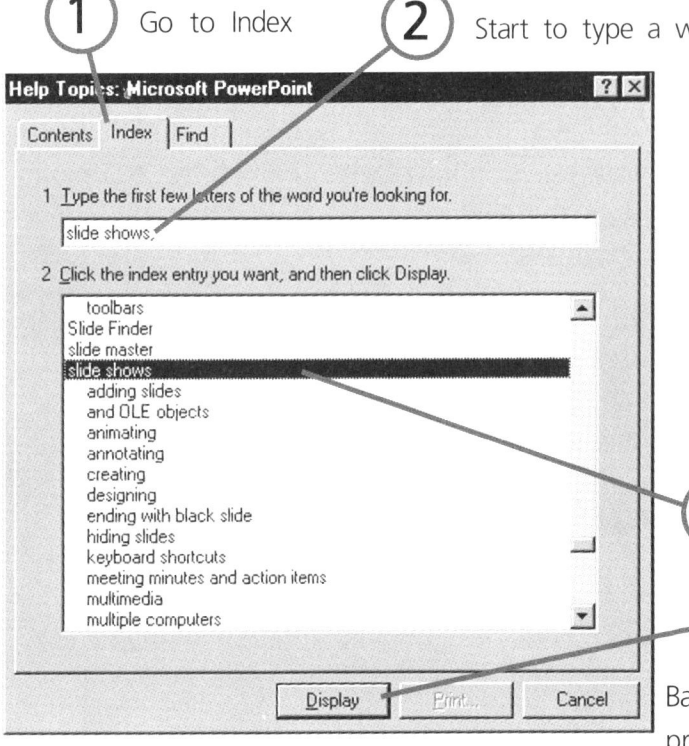

Go to Index

Start to type a word

Select an entry

Click Display

Back to the previous page

Options include one to print the topic

Go to the Help Topics dialog box

Work through to the required Help

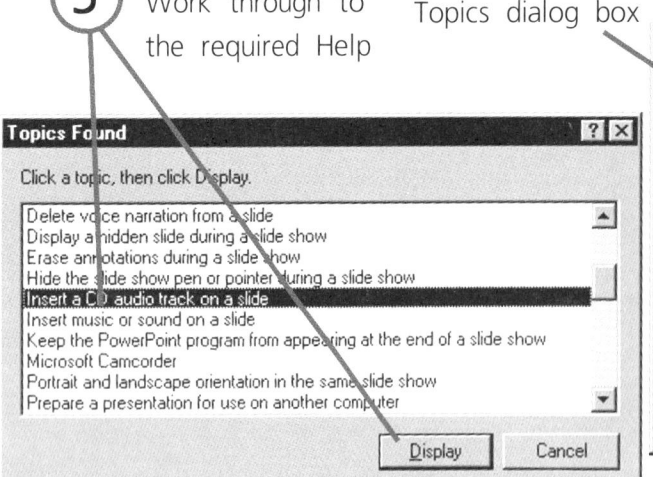

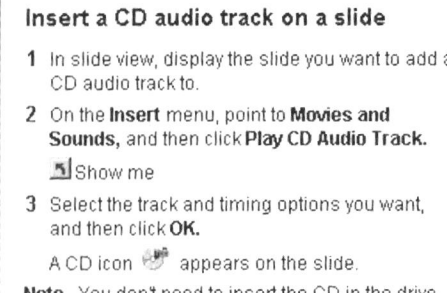

Basic steps

Find tab

1 Select the **Find** tab. The first time you use it, a wizard runs to set up your word list.

2 Type in your word (or part of it – enough to get some matching words displayed).

3 Select a matching word to narrow the search.

4 Choose a topic.

5 Click [Display].

6 Close the Help when you are done.

Use the Find tab to search out specific words and phrases, rather than look for a particular category of information.

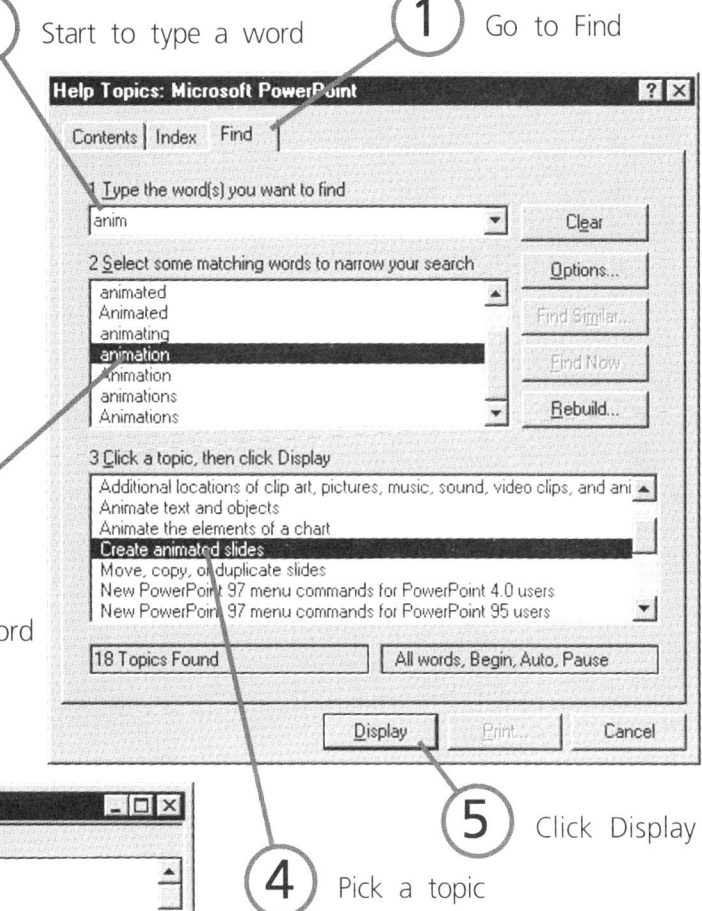

② Start to type a word ① Go to Find

③ Pick a word

④ Pick a topic

⑤ Click Display

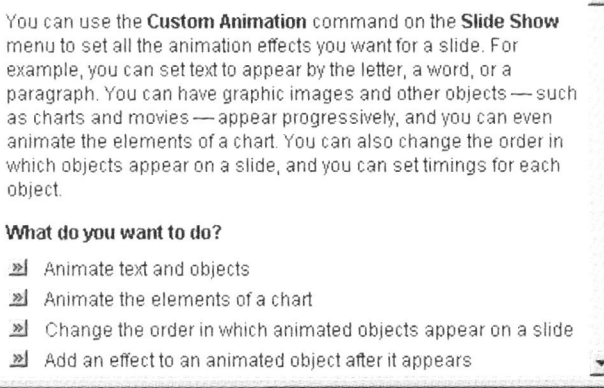

Create animated slides

You can use the **Custom Animation** command on the **Slide Show** menu to set all the animation effects you want for a slide. For example, you can set text to appear by the letter, a word, or a paragraph. You can have graphic images and other objects — such as charts and movies — appear progressively, and you can even animate the elements of a chart. You can also change the order in which objects appear on a slide, and you can set timings for each object.

What do you want to do?

» Animate text and objects

» Animate the elements of a chart

» Change the order in which animated objects appear on a slide

» Add an effect to an animated object after it appears

Tip

This is not the easiest way to get help if you're new to PowerPoint. It can be hard to find help on 'simple' things!

Summary

❏ Press **[F1]** or click the Office Assistant tool [?] to get help with your tasks.

❏ Use the **What's this?** feature to check out menu items, tools and buttons on your screen.

❏ The **Office Assistant** can have its appearance and behaviour customised.

❏ **ScreenTips** are useful learning aids when you start out using PowerPoint.

❏ Choose **Contents and Index** from the Help Menu and browse through the on-line help pages from the **Contents** tab.

❏ **Search** for specific categories of information from the **Index** tab.

❏ Locate help on specific words using the **Find** tab.

3 The new presentation

AutoContent Wizard

In this section we will look at the different options for creating a presentation – we will consider its content later. Whichever option you select, you still end up creating slides, notes and handouts for your presentation.

The easiest way to create your first presentation is to use the AutoContent Wizard. The wizard helps you set up the Title Slide (the first slide in your presentation), and gives you an outline to follow as you build up the other slides.

Basic steps

1 Start up PowerPoint and go to the PowerPoint dialog box.

2 Select the **AutoContent Wizard.**

3 Click [OK].

4 The first time you run this wizard the Office Assistant dashes to your aid! Close the Assistant if you wish and click [Next>].

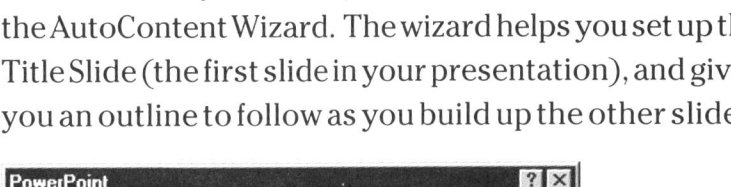

③ Click OK

② Select AutoContent Wizard

Close Office Assistant

Take note

Several slides will be set up – how many depends on the choices you make as you work through the Wizard.

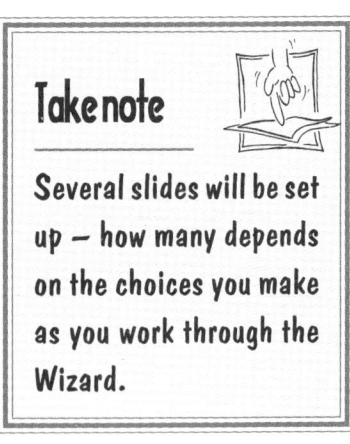

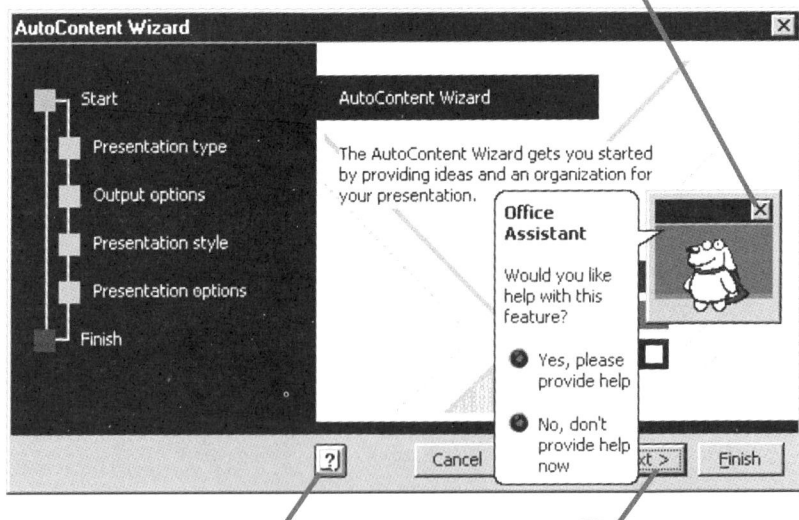

You can call up the Office Assistant at any time

④ Click Next

5 Pick the option that best describes the type of presentation you are going to give.

6 Choose the Output option for the Presentation.

cont...

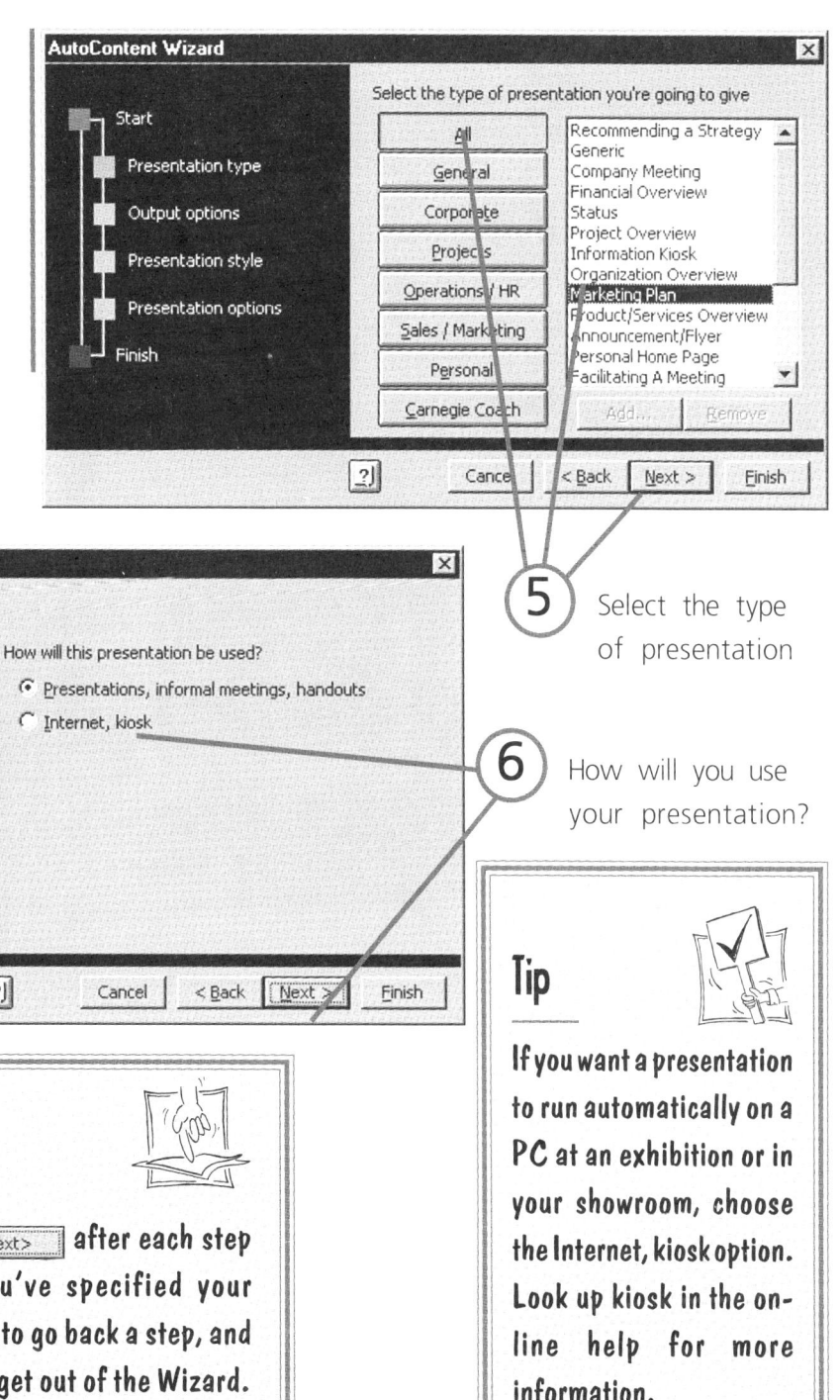

(5) Select the type of presentation

(6) How will you use your presentation?

Tip

If you want a presentation to run automatically on a PC at an exhibition or in your showroom, choose the Internet, kiosk option. Look up kiosk in the on-line help for more information.

Take note

In any Wizard, click [Next>] after each step and [Finish] once you've specified your options. Click [<Back] to go back a step, and [Cancel] if you want to get out of the Wizard.

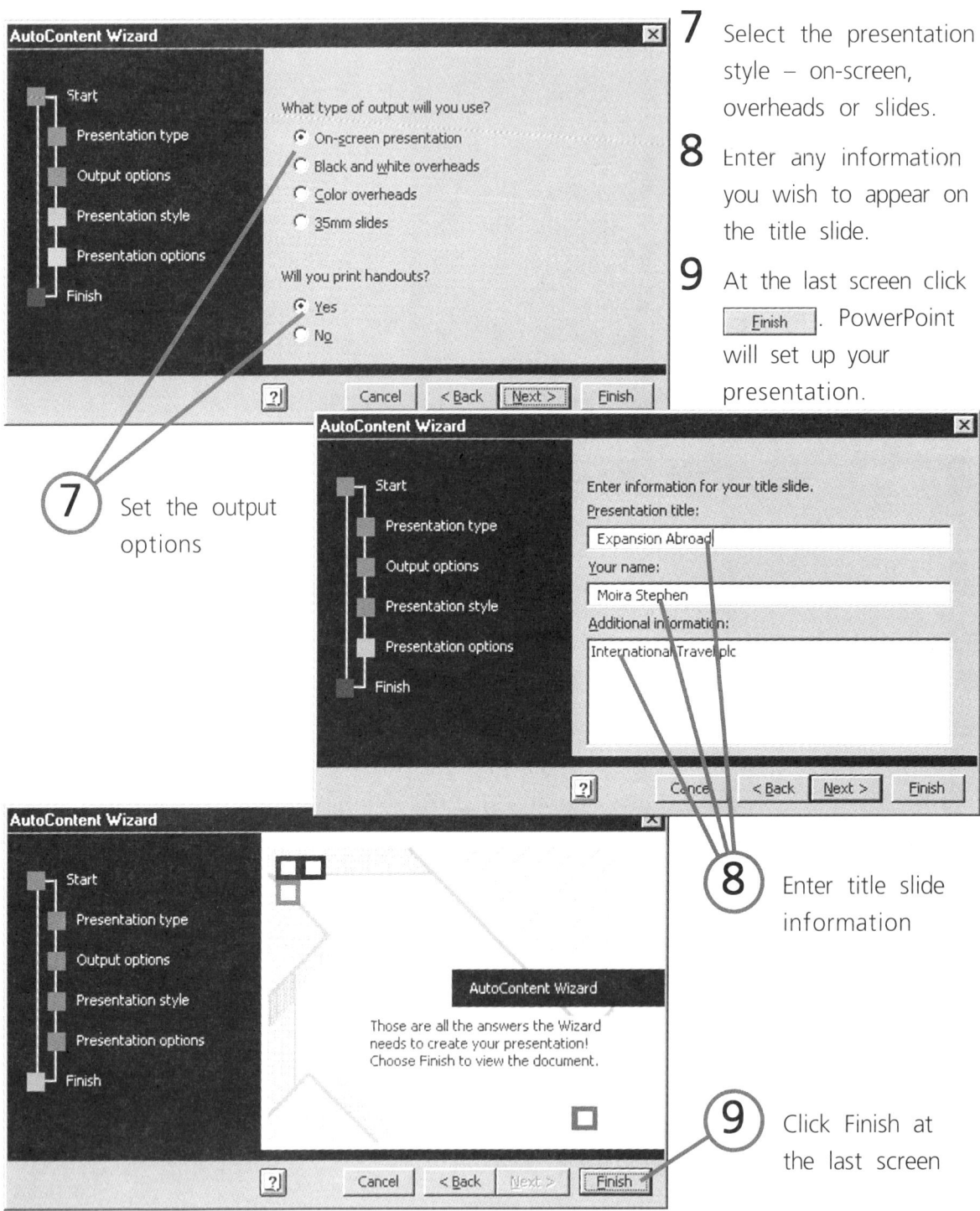

7 Select the presentation style – on-screen, overheads or slides.

8 Enter any information you wish to appear on the title slide.

9 At the last screen click [Finish]. PowerPoint will set up your presentation.

⑦ Set the output options

⑧ Enter title slide information

⑨ Click Finish at the last screen

❑ Your presentation is displayed in Outline view – see Chapter 4.

You can easily change to Slide view if your prefer. Click the Slide view button in the bottom left of the window.

Slide icons

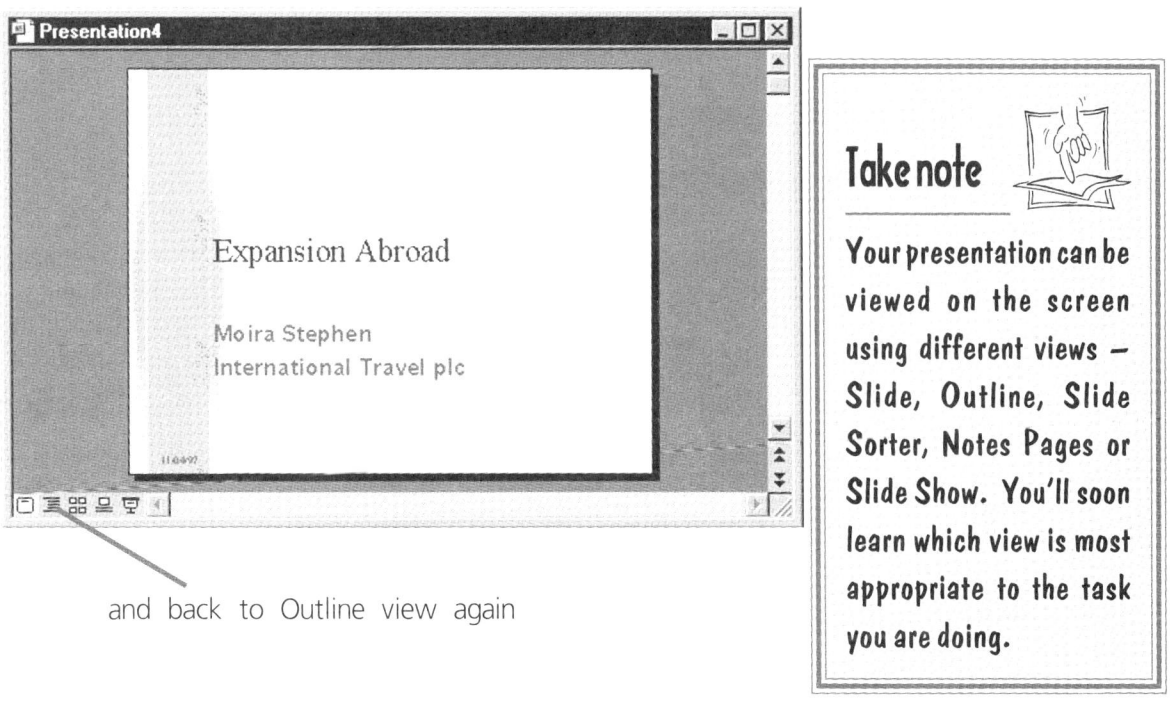

Change to Slide view if you wish

and back to Outline view again

Take note

Your presentation can be viewed on the screen using different views – Slide, Outline, Slide Sorter, Notes Pages or Slide Show. You'll soon learn which view is most appropriate to the task you are doing.

Template

This option lets you start out by choosing the template on which you wish to base your presentation. The template will determine the design elements of your presentation, including font and colour scheme.

Basic steps

1 At the PowerPoint dialog box select the **Template** option.

2 Click [OK].

3 Choose the Presentation design you wish to use from the **New Presentation** dialog box.

4 Click [OK].

❑ If you select from the **Presentations** tab, you are taken directly to the title slide of your presentation. Stop here!

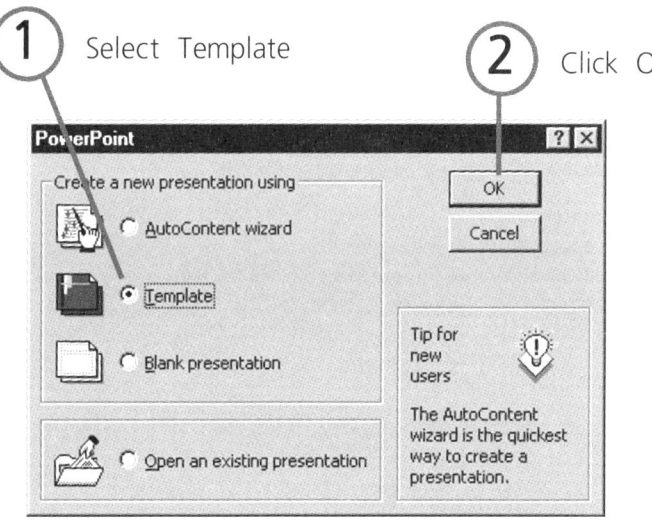

① Select Template

② Click OK

Select from either tab

③ Choose a design

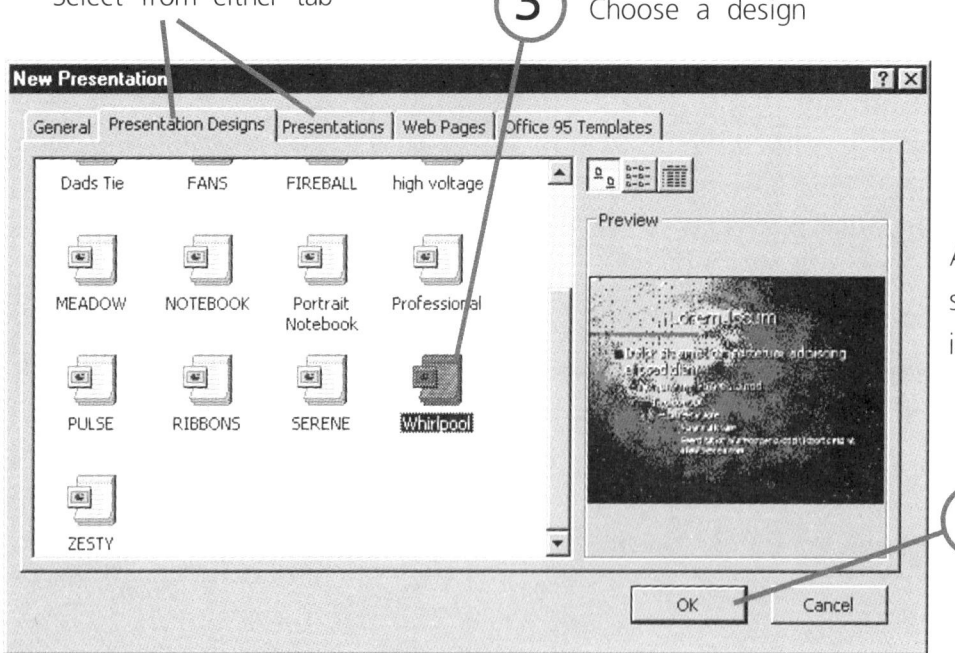

A preview of the selected design is displayed here

④ Click OK

❑ If you select from the **Presentation Designs** tab, you are taken to the New Slide dialog box to choose a layout for the first slide.

5 Select a layout.

6 Click [OK].

❑ Once PowerPoint has set up the presentation, it displays it in Slide view. The first slide is displayed, ready for your input.

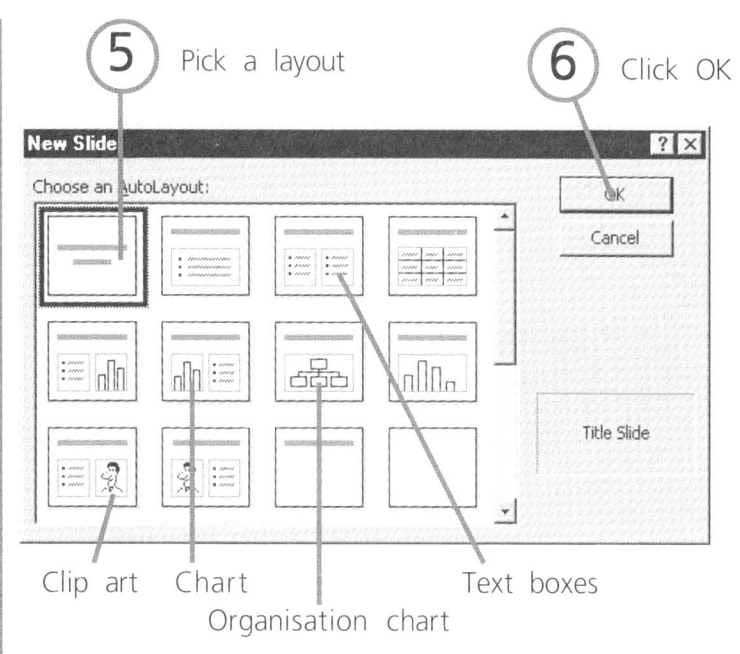

⑤ Pick a layout

⑥ Click OK

Clip art   Chart

Organisation chart

Text boxes

Take note

If you don't like the look of your slides with the template you select, change it. Double click on the template name on the status bar. This takes you to the **Apply Design Template** dialog box where you can select a different template.

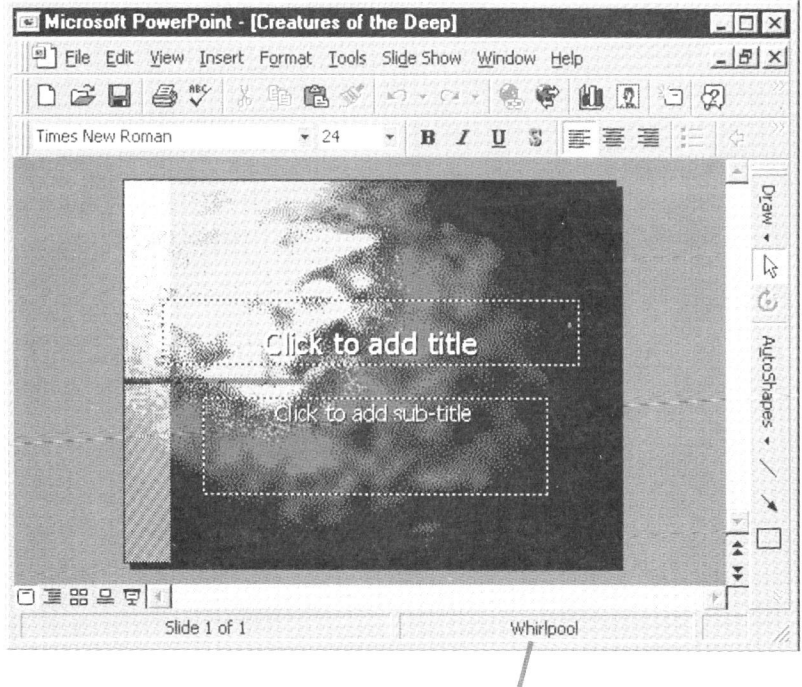

Current Template – double click here to change

Blank Presentation

If you prefer to set up your own presentation try the Blank Presentation. The colour scheme, fonts and other design features are set to the default values when you choose this option.

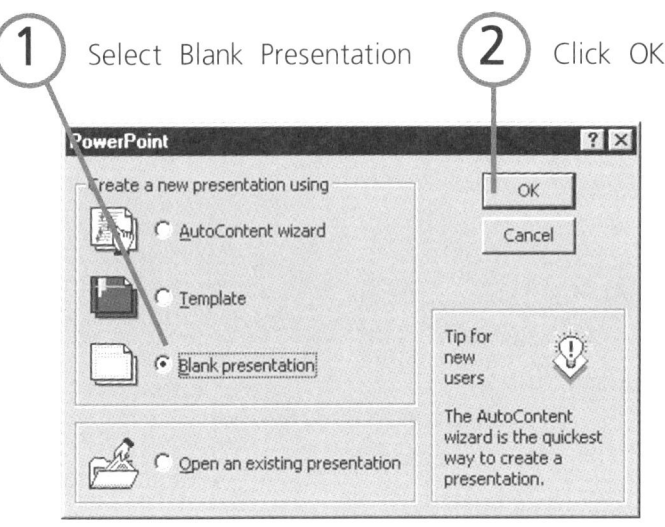

① Select Blank Presentation ② Click OK

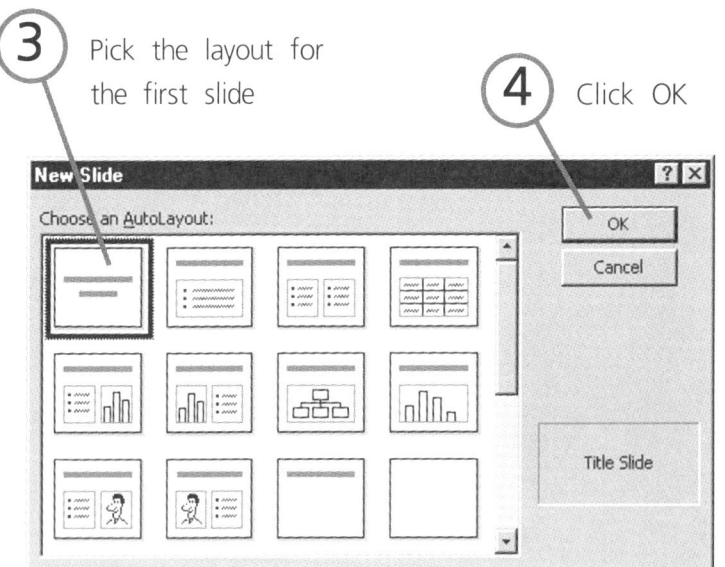

③ Pick the layout for the first slide

④ Click OK

1 At the PowerPoint dialog box select the **Blank Presentation** option.

2 Click ⌗ OK ⌗.

3 Choose a slide layout for your first slide – usually the title slide.

4 Click ⌗ OK ⌗.

❏ Once PowerPoint has set up the presentation, it displays it in Slide view. The slide you chose at step 3 is displayed, ready for your input.

Take note

Some of the slide layouts in the New Slide dialog box have graphic, table, organisation chart and clip art objects set up on them. We will look at these later in the book.

Slide ready for completion

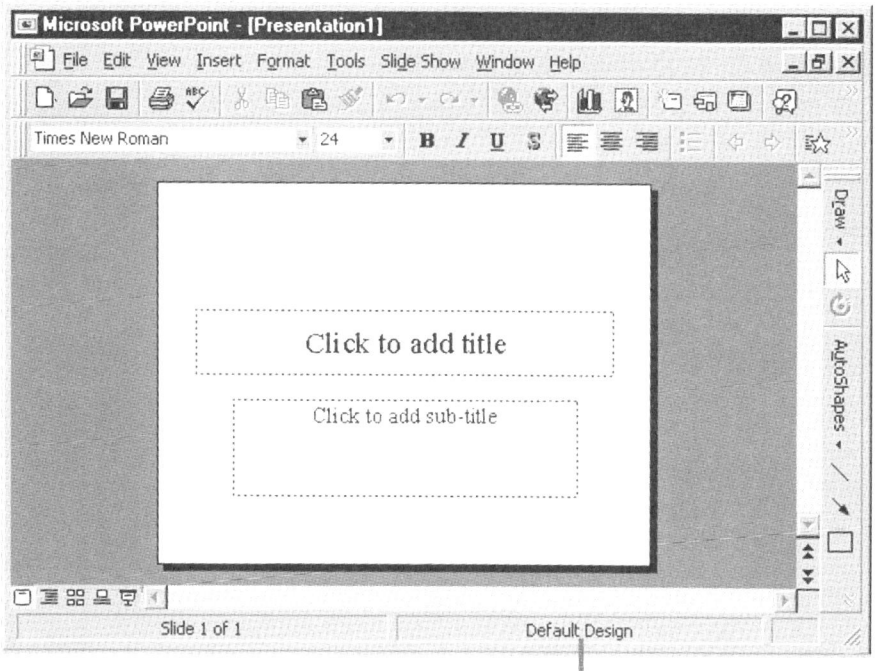

Double click here to add a design template later, if wanted

Tip

If you don't like the structured approach of the AutoContent Wizard, you may find the 'clean' look created by the Blank Presentation option easiest to work with in the early stages of setting up your presentation. The colours, templates and patterns can all be applied later.

Take note

The boxes with dotted outlines that appear when you create a new slide are called placeholders.

Different slide layouts have different placeholders set up on them - the placeholders will contain the slide title, slide text and any other objects you display on your slide.

Starting within PowerPoint

Basic steps

The PowerPoint dialog box is not the only place from which you can create a new presentation. When working in PowerPoint you can create a new one any time.

1 Open the **File** menu.

2 Choose **New**.

3 At the **New Presentation** dialog box select a template for your presentation from either the **General**, **Presentations** or **Presentation Designs** tab.

4 Specify the **AutoLayout** (only needed from the General or Presentation Designs tabs).

5 Click [OK].

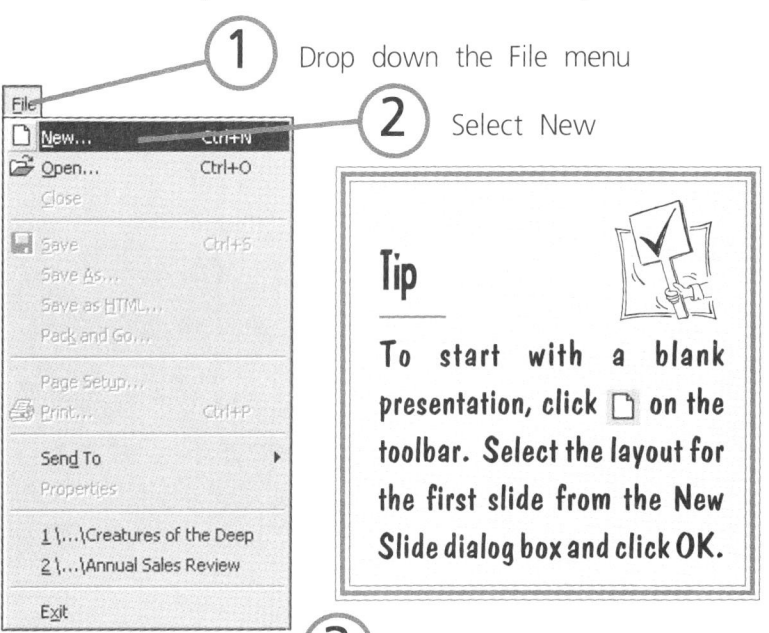

① Drop down the File menu

② Select New

Tip

To start with a blank presentation, click ☐ on the toolbar. Select the layout for the first slide from the New Slide dialog box and click OK.

③ Select a Presentation

④ If necessary choose a layout

⑤ Click OK

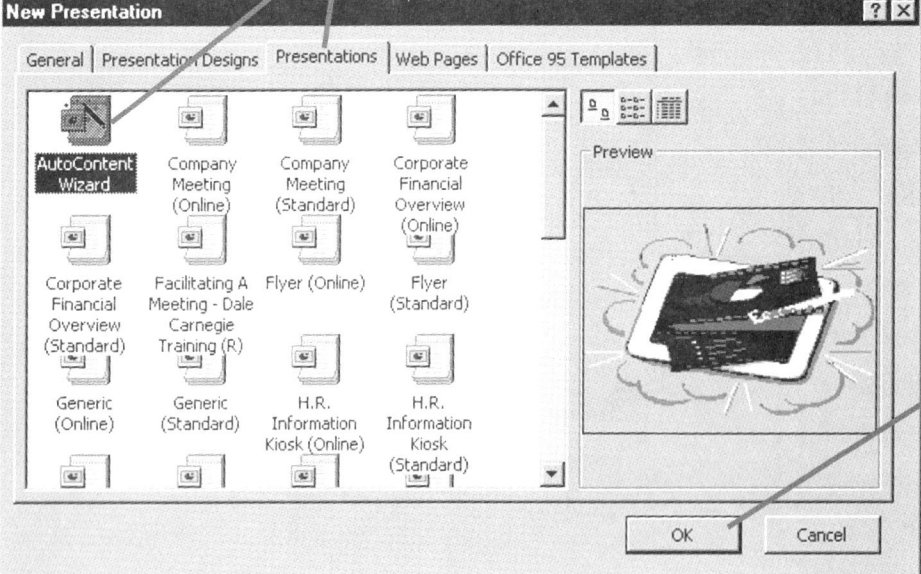

28

Basic steps

1 Click 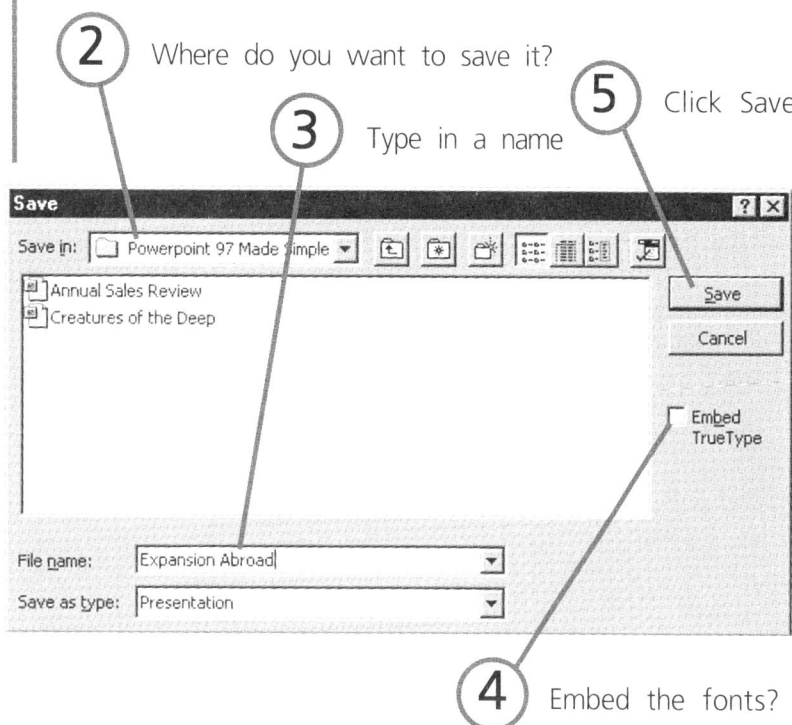 the **Save** tool on the Standard toolbar.

2 Specify the **Drive** and/ or **Folder** into which you wish to save your presentation.

3 Give your presentation a **File name**.

4 If the presentation is to be viewed on a system that does not have your fonts, select **Embed True Type**. The fonts are then saved in the presentation file.

5 Click ⬚ Save ⬚.

Once you have set up your presentation, you must save it if you want to keep it (if you don't save it, it will be lost when you close PowerPoint or switch off your computer).

(2) Where do you want to save it?

(3) Type in a name

(5) Click Save

(4) Embed the fonts?

Save vs Save As

The first time you save a presentation, you are taken to the **Save** dialog box to give it a name and specify the folder and drive you want it saved in. Thereafter, any time you save the presentation using the **Save** tool 🖫 on the toolbar, the old version of the file is replaced by the new, edited version. This is what you would usually want to happen.

However, if you have saved your presentation, gone on to edit it, then wish to save the edited version using a different filename, or in a different location, open the **File** menu and choose **Save As** to get to the **Save** dialog box.

Closing down

When you've finished working on your presentation you must save it (see previous page) and close it.

Leaving PowerPoint is very easy. If you use other Windows packages, the technique is very similar.

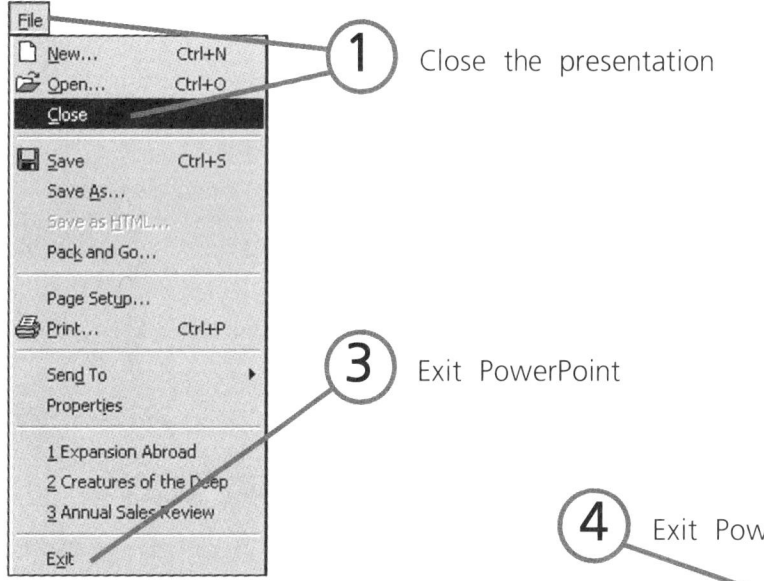

① Close the presentation

③ Exit PowerPoint

❏ **Closing a presentation**

1 Open the **File** Menu and choose **Close**.

or

2 Click the **Close** button on the **Presentation** title bar.

❏ **Leaving PowerPoint**

3 Open the **File** Menu and choose **Exit**.

or

4 Click the **Close** button on the **PowerPoint** title bar.

④ Exit PowerPoint

② Close the presentation

Take note

If you have made changes to your presentation since you last saved it, you will be prompted to save your changes before the file is closed. If you want to save the changes, choose Yes at the prompt.

Opening a presentation

1 Click ![icon] the Open tool on the Standard toolbar.

or

2 Open the **File** menu and choose **Open**.

3 Select the **Drive** and **Folder** that contains your presentation file.

4 Select the presentation.

5 Click [Open].

If you want to work on a presentation you've already created, saved and closed, you must open it first.

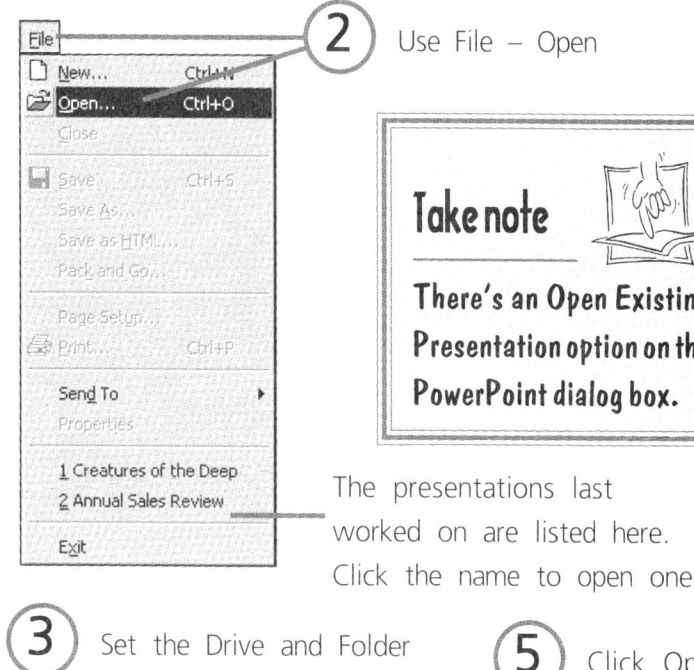

② Use File – Open

Take note

There's an Open Existing Presentation option on the PowerPoint dialog box.

The presentations last worked on are listed here. Click the name to open one.

Tip

You can open a presentation by double clicking its name.

③ Set the Drive and Folder

④ Select the file

⑤ Click Open

Preview of first slide in selected presentation

Open

Look in: Powerpoint 97 Made Simple

Name
- Annual Sales Review
- Creatures of the Deep
- Expansion Abroad

Open
Cancel
Advanced...

Find files that match these search criteria:

File name: ▢
Text or property: ▢
Find Now

Files of type: Presentations and Shows
Last modified: any time
New Search

3 file(s) found.

31

Summary

❏ When creating a **new presentation**, you can choose your starting point – the AutoContent Wizard, a template or a Blank rresentation.

❏ The easiest/quickest option for your first presentation is probably the **AutoContent Wizard**, where you begin with a presentation that contains suggested content and design.

❏ The colour scheme, background objects, bullets, fonts, etc. are set up in the presentation **template**.

❏ Start with a **Blank presentation** if you prefer to set up your own design, or apply a template later.

❏ The **first slide** of your presentation is displayed once you have specified your options.

❏ Regardless of the options selected when you create your presentation, you can easily **change any option** as your presentation develops.

❏ Use the **Save** tool on the Standard Toolbar to save your presentation.

❏ Click the **Close** button on the presentation title bar to close the file.

❏ To **Exit** PowerPoint, click the Close button on the top title bar.

❏ Use the file name list in the File menu to open a **recently used presentation.**

❏ To create a new presentation from within PowerPoint, choose **New** from the **File** menu.

4 Outline view

Setting up the outline

Once you've passed the initial stages, the next step is usually to decide on the text you want on your slides – the title, and the main points to cover during your presentation. You can add text in either Outline view or Slide view.

In Outline view you can work on your text without the distraction of colour, graphics, etc. You can also determine the structure of the text on each slide (main points, sub-points, etc), using up to 5 levels if necessary.

Slide Title

Level 1
    Level 2
        Level 3
            Level 4
                Level 5

If you create your presentation using the AutoContent Wizard, you are taken into Outline view. If you create a presentation using one of the other options you are taken into Slide view. You can move from one view to the other using the tools at the bottom left of the screen.

View tools

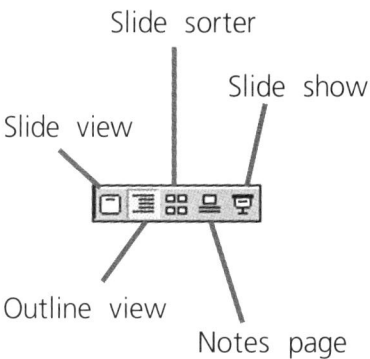

Slide sorter

Slide show

Slide view

Outline view

Notes page

The Outlining Toolbar

The Outlining toolbar is usually displayed down the left-hand side of the screen.

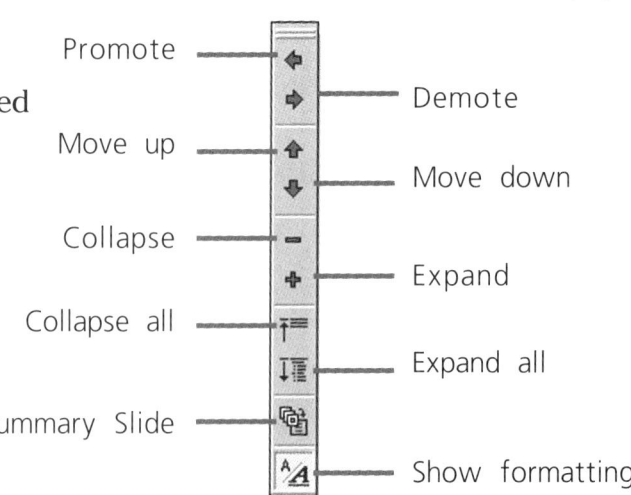

Promote

Demote

Move up

Move down

Collapse

Expand

Collapse all

Expand all

Summary Slide

Show formatting

Basic steps

1 Position the insertion point or select the text you want to replace.

2 Key in you own text.

3 Should you wish to make a list of points, simply press **[Enter]** after each point to move onto a new line.

Take note

If you opt to close the slide miniature, you can open it again from the View menu.

If you used the AutoContent Wizard it will have set up a number of slides for you, with each given a Slide Title. Suggestions on the points you might want to make on each slide are also given. These should be replaced with your own points. (You can also change the Slide Title.)

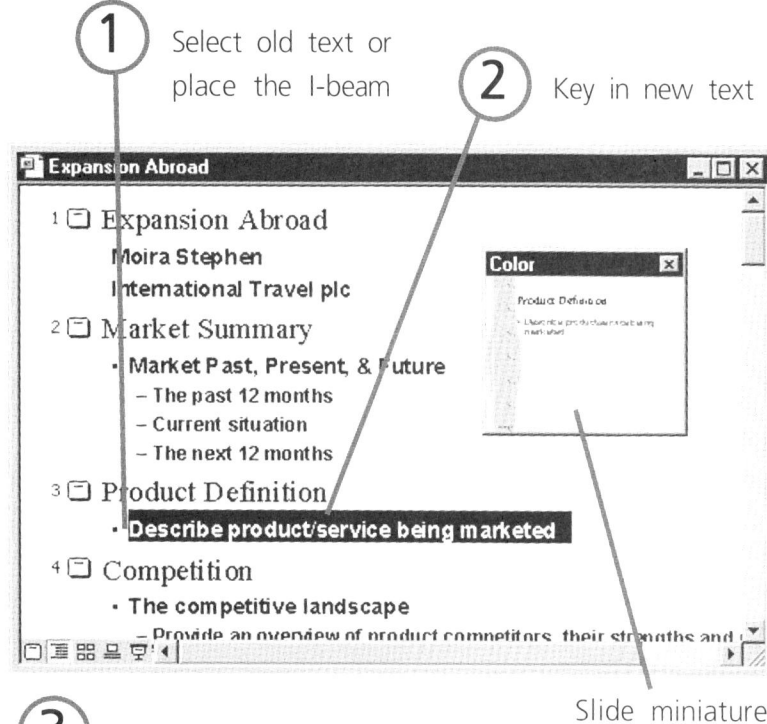

① Select old text or place the I-beam

② Key in new text

Slide miniature

③ Press [Enter] for a new item

Selecting in Outline view

- **Click and Drag**
- **[Shift]-Click:** place the insertion point at one end of the text, move the I beam to the other end, hold down **[Shift]** and click the left mouse button.
- To select a point: single click on the bullet to the left of the point (note special 4-pointed mouse pointer) or double click to the right of the point.
- To select a whole slide: single click on the slide icon to the left of the slide.

New slides

Regardless of how you create your presentation, you will need to add new slides at some stage. You can add new slides at any place in your presentation (not just at the end). In Outline view, you would most likely want to add Bulleted list layout slides, although you can use any layout you wish. As you can only add text in Outline view, should you select a layout that contains a different type of object (see page 6), you must change views to enter it.

Try adding in a new slide in Outline view.

1 Position the insertion point inside the slide that you want to be above your new one.

2 Click 🖫 the **New Slide** tool, or press [Ctrl]-[M].

3 Select a layout.

4 Click ⬜ OK ⬜.

(1) Select the preceding slide

(2) Click the New Slide tool

(3) Select a layout

New Slide   ? ✕

Choose an AutoLayout:

     OK

     Cancel

Bulleted List

(4) Click OK

Describes the selected layout

Take note

Once you have keyed in the slide title, pressing [Enter] creates a new slide using the bulleted list layout. If you wish to list some points under the slide title, you must demote to move into the next level – see Promoting and Demoting (page 38).

Tip

The keyboard shortcut [Ctrl]-[M] opens the New Slide dialog box.

New slide

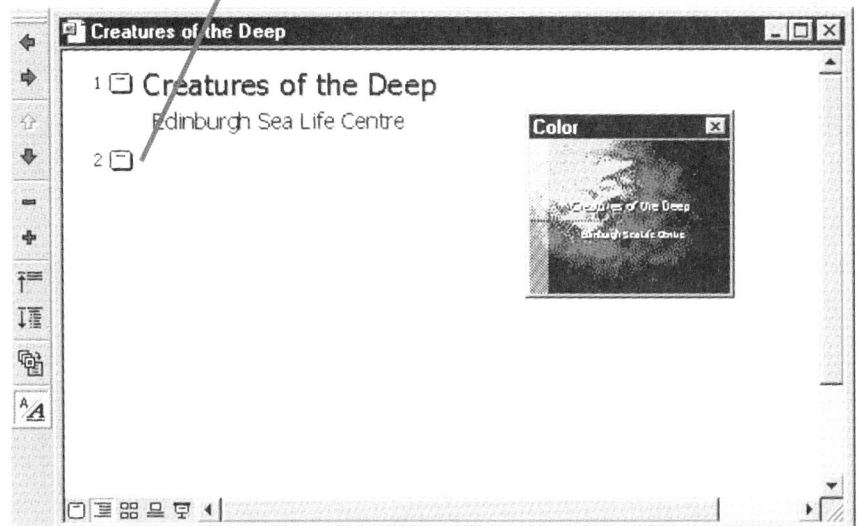

After text added –
note the bullet
points

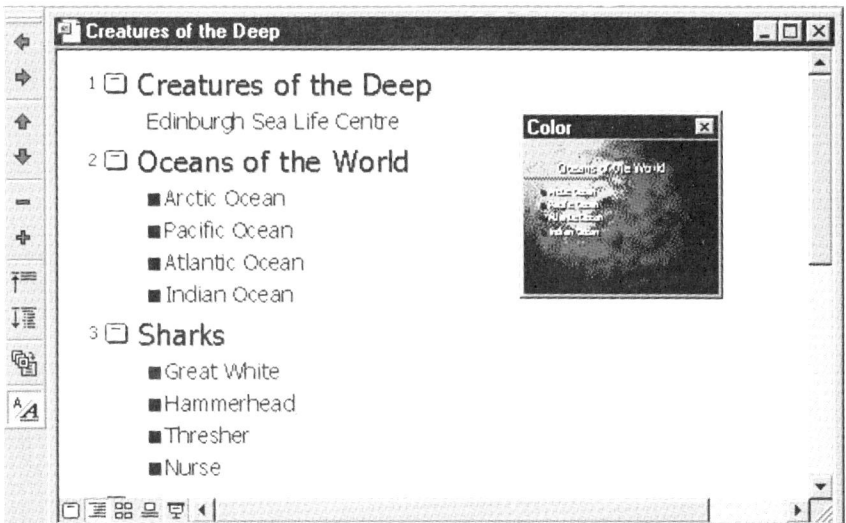

Take note

If you press [Enter] at the end of any slide in Outline view, you can demote (see next page) back to the Slide Title level where a new slide (in the same layout as the preceding slide) will be created.

Promoting and demoting

The points you want to make on your slides will be structured – you will have main points (at the first bulleted level) and some of these points will have sub-points (at the second, third, fourth or even fifth level).

Initially, all points on your slide are at level 1. You can easily demote sub items if necessary (and promote them again if you change your mind).

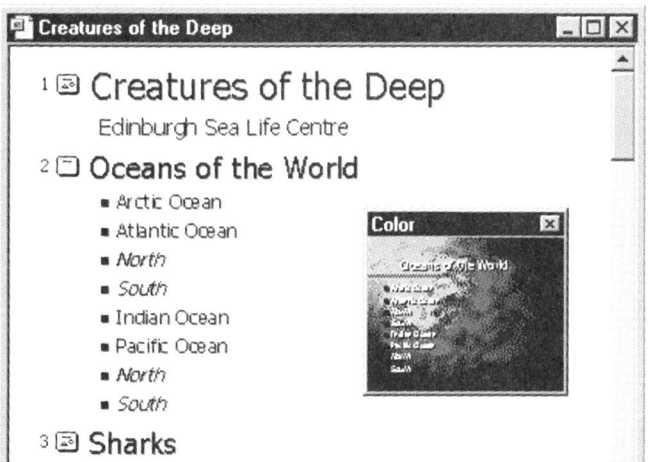

Basic steps

1 Place the insertion point in the item.

❏ **To demote an item**

2 Click ➡ the Demote tool on the Outlining (or Formatting) toolbar.

❏ **To promote an item**

2 Click ⬅ the Promote tool.

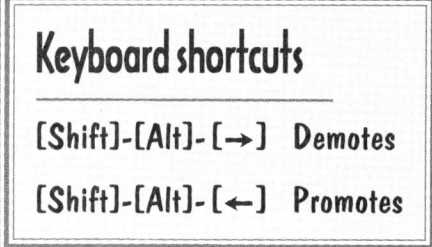

Keyboard shortcuts

[Shift]-[Alt]-[→]   Demotes

[Shift]-[Alt]-[←]   Promotes

These items have been demoted

Take note

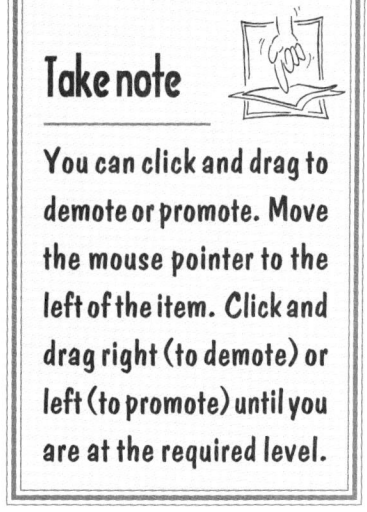

You can click and drag to demote or promote. Move the mouse pointer to the left of the item. Click and drag right (to demote) or left (to promote) until you are at the required level.

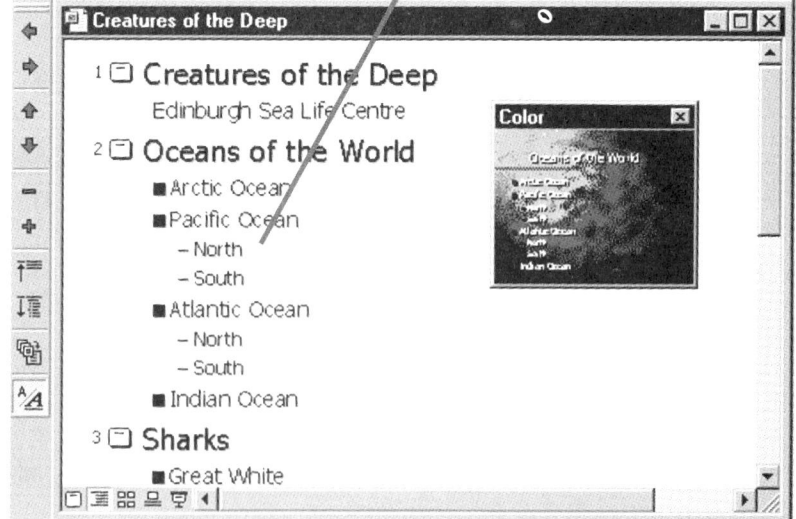

Basic steps

❑ **Collapse selected slides**

1 Highlight the set, or place the insertion point anywhere within a single slide.

2 Click ⊟ the **Collapse** tool.

❑ **To expand again**

3 Select the title(s).

4 Click ⊞ the **Expand** tool.

❑ **All the slides**

5 Click ⊤≣ the **Collapse All** tool on the Outlining toolbar.

6 To expand your presentation again, click ⊥≣ the **Expand All** tool.

If you want to get an overview of your presentation, or part of your presentation, you can collapse all (or part of) the outline down to show just the Slide Titles. The outline can then be expanded again to show the text as required.

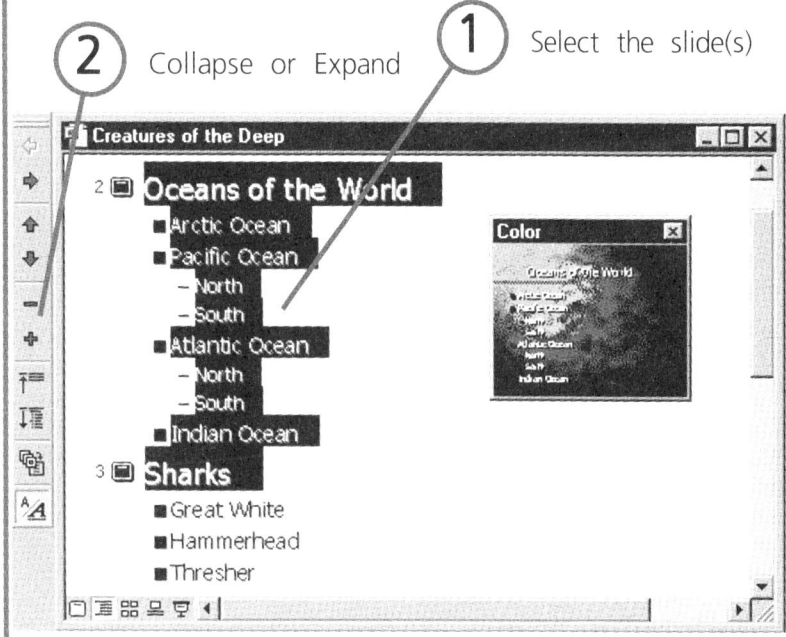

② Collapse or Expand   ① Select the slide(s)

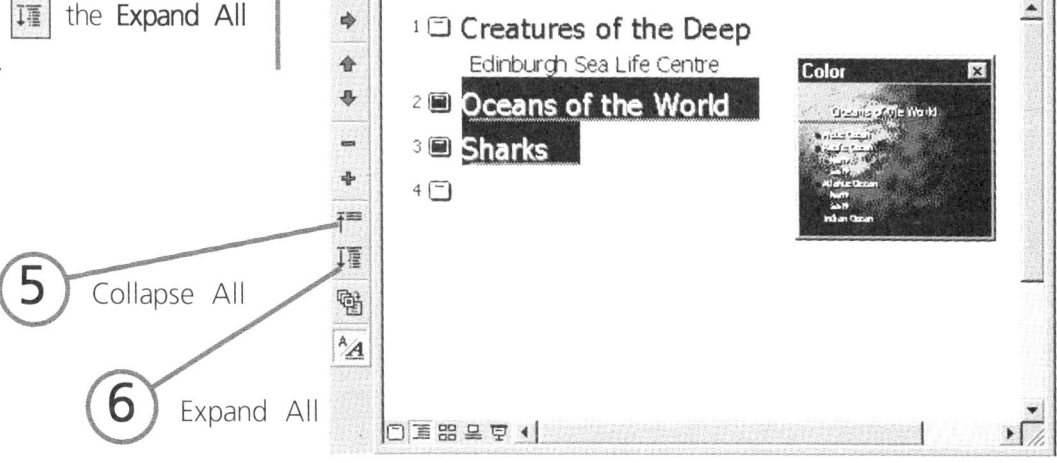

⑤ Collapse All

⑥ Expand All

Rearranging an outline

If you decide that you want to change the order of the points you have made, this is very easily done in Outline view.

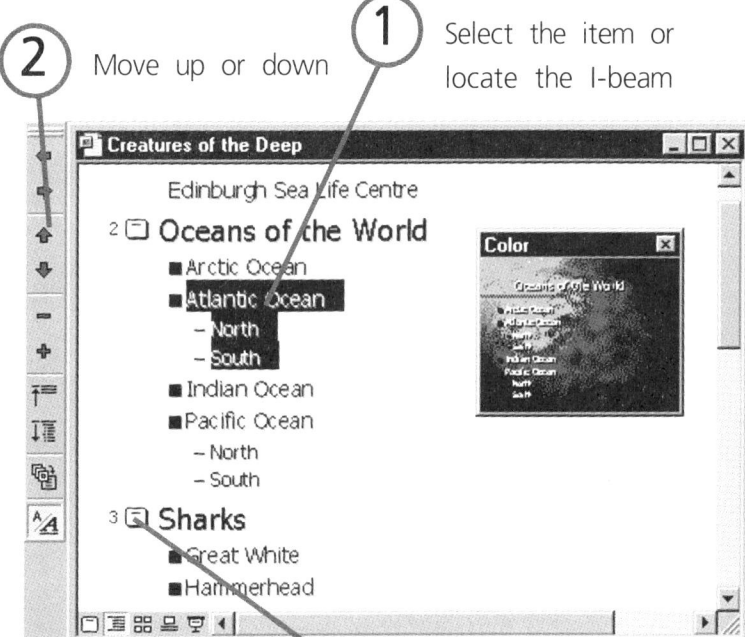

② Move up or down

① Select the item or locate the I-beam

③ Click on the icon

Basic steps

❑ **Moving items**

1 Select, or place the insertion point in the item you wish to move.

2 Click ⬆ the Move Up tool to move it up through the slide(s) .

or

Click ⬇ the Move Down tool to move it down through the slide(s).

❑ **Moving slides**

3 Click on the slide icon to the left of the one you want to move.

4 Use the tools, mouse or keyboard to move the whole slide to its new location.

Keyboard shortcuts

[Shift]-[Alt]-[↑]   moves an item up

[Shift]-[Alt]-[↓]   moves an item down

Basic steps

1 Click the slide icon on the left of the title to select the slide.

2 Press [Delete].

❏ If the slide you try to delete contains objects other than text, e.g. clip art, movies, etc, you will be asked to confirm the deletion.

If you need to remove a slide it can easily be deleted in Outline view.

① Click to select the slide

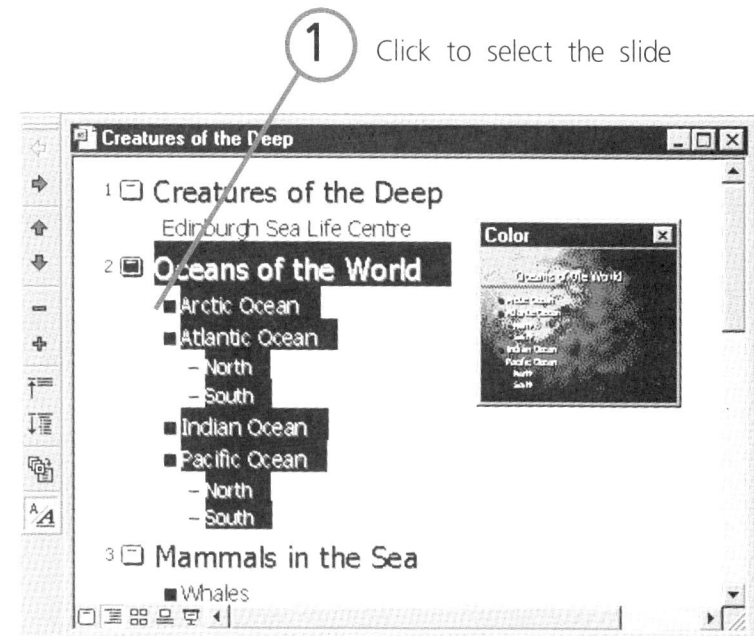

Take note

You can delete slides in Outline view, Slide view, Slide Sorter view or Notes Page view.

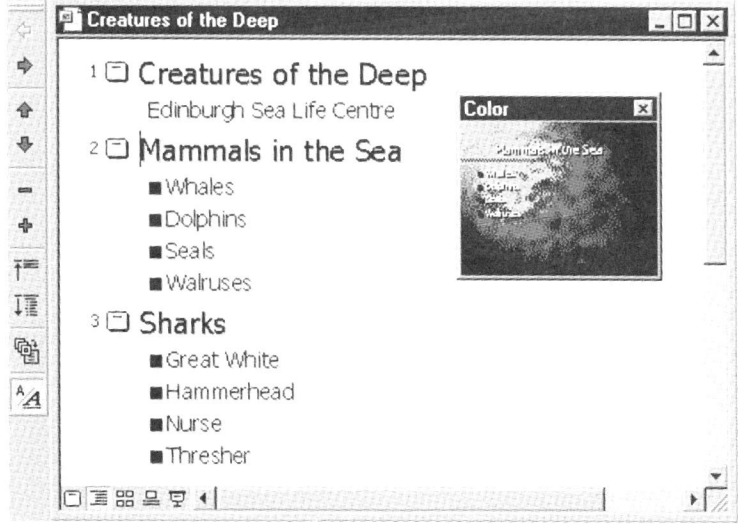

Take note

If you want to delete a slide in Slide or Notes Page view, you must view the slide then choose Delete Slide from the View menu.

Summary

❑ **Outline view** lets you concentrate on the text and structure of your presentation.

❑ In Outline view, you can specify the **slide title** and the **points** you wish to make on each slide.

❑ **New slides** can be added at any place in your presentation.

❑ Your points can contain sub-points if necessary (up to 5 **levels**).

❑ You cannot add **pictures**, **charts** etc in Outline view.

❑ Using an outline, you can **collapse** and **expand** your presentation to show the slides required.

❑ You can move between Outline view and the **other views** whenever you wish.

❑ You can **rearrange** the order or **delete** slides in Outline – or any other – view.

5   Working in Slide view

Slide view

You can move between the different views at any time. Use whatever view seems most appropriate to what you are doing. Once you appreciate what you can do in the different views, you can decide for yourself which you need to use. In this section we will look at the ways you can work in Slide view. You can add text, graphics, clip art, tables, charts and media clips in Slide view. We'll stick to text for the time being.

If you're still in Outline view, change to Slide view for this section.

Basic steps

1 Place the insertion point in the slide you want to look.

2 Click the Slide view tool.

Or

3 Double click the icon beside the title of the slide you want to see in Slide view.

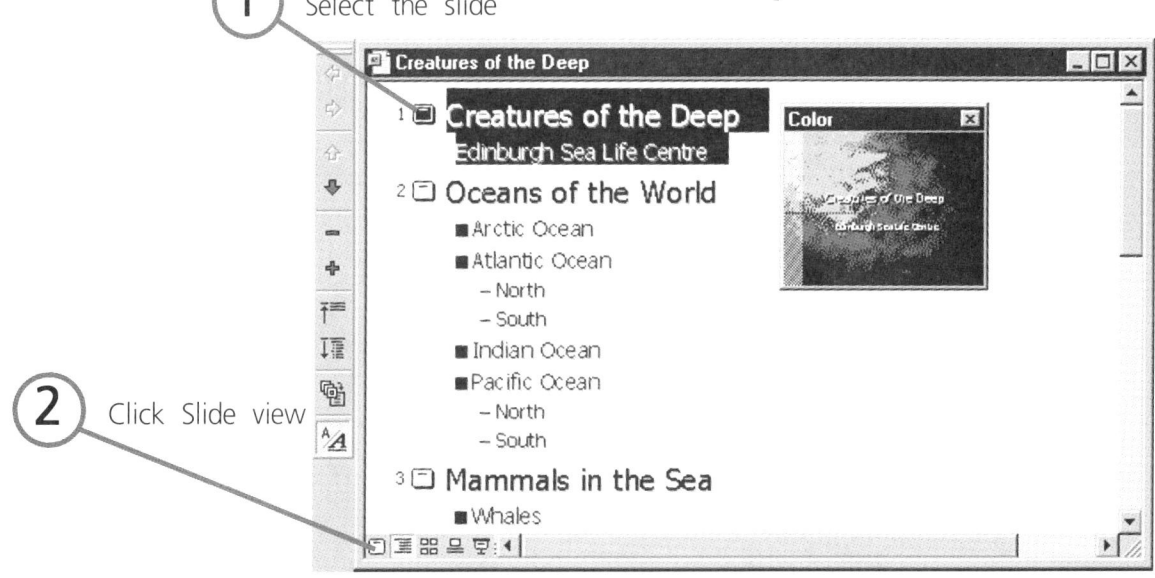

① Select the slide

② Click Slide view

Take note

When creating your slides you usually work in either Outline or Slide view.

* In Outline view, you can only enter text

* In Slide view, you can also enter clip art, organisation charts, graphs etc.

Basic steps

Moving between slides

1 Drag the elevator up or down the scroll bar to display the desired slide.

2 Note the slide number and presentation name that appears when you drag the elevator. Release the mouse button, when you reach the desired slide.

or

3 Click the **Previous Slide** button to move up.

4 Click the **Next Slide** button to move down.

In Slide view, you see one slide at a time on your screen. When you have several slides, you must move up or down through them to view them.

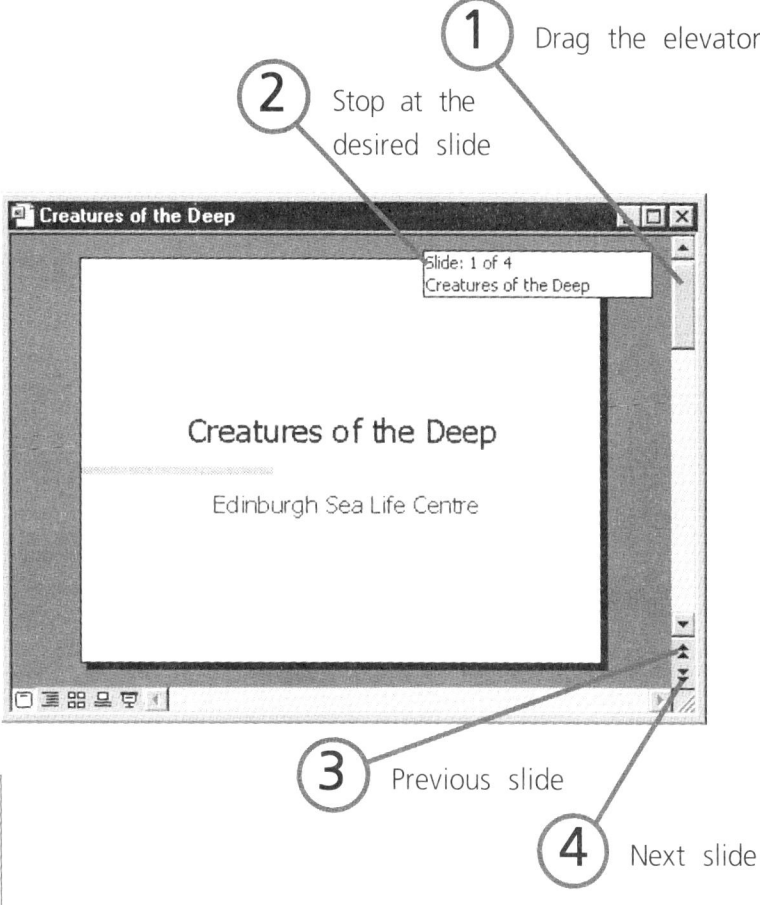

① Drag the elevator

② Stop at the desired slide

③ Previous slide

④ Next slide

Take note

You can move from one view to another at any time.

Keyboard shortcuts

Press [Page Up] to move to the previous slide

[Page Down] to move to the next slide.

Adding new slides

As your presentation develops you may need to add more slides to it. It doesn't matter how you created your presentation – using the AutoContent Wizard, a template or a blank presentation – new slides can easily be added at any place as required.

① Go to the slide above the new one

③ Select a layout　④ Click OK

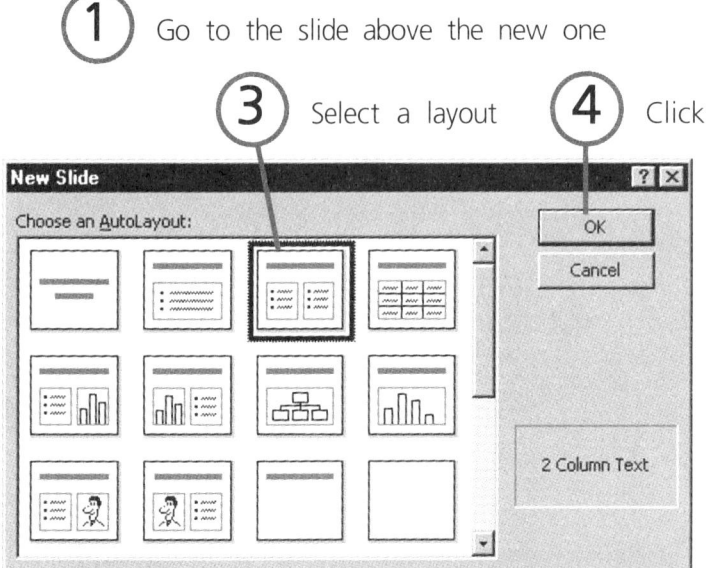

Basic steps

1 View the slide that will be above your new one.

2 Click  the **New Slide** tool on the Standard toolbar.

3 Select the slide layout required from the **New Slide** dialog box.

4 Click [OK].

Take note

You can add slides in Outline view, Slide view, Slide Sorter view or Notes Pages view.

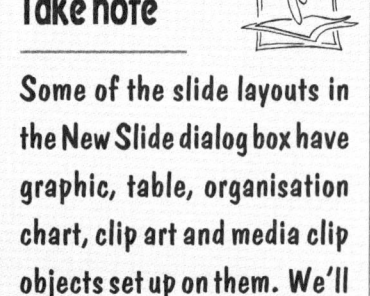

Take note

Some of the slide layouts in the New Slide dialog box have graphic, table, organisation chart, clip art and media clip objects set up on them. We'll look at these later in the book.

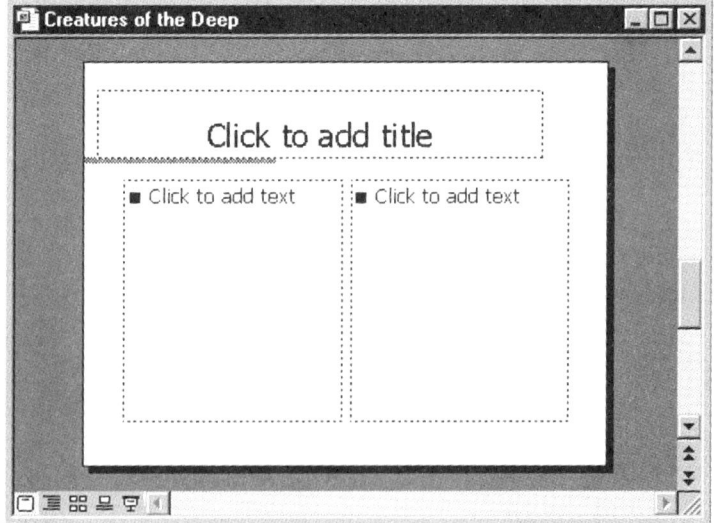

Entering and editing text

❏ **Adding text**

1 Click in the title area.

2 Key in your text.

3 Click in the bulleted list placeholder.

4 Key in your text and press **[Enter]** after each item.

5 Repeat step 4 until all your points are listed.

❏ **Editing text**

1 Locate the slide you wish to edit.

2 Click to place the insertion point inside the text to be edited.

3 Insert or delete characters as required.

To enter text into a slide you have just added, simply follow the instructions on the slide!

To edit text on an existing slide, you must first locate the slide you wish to edit, then make the changes required. To edit the text, use the normal Windows techniques.

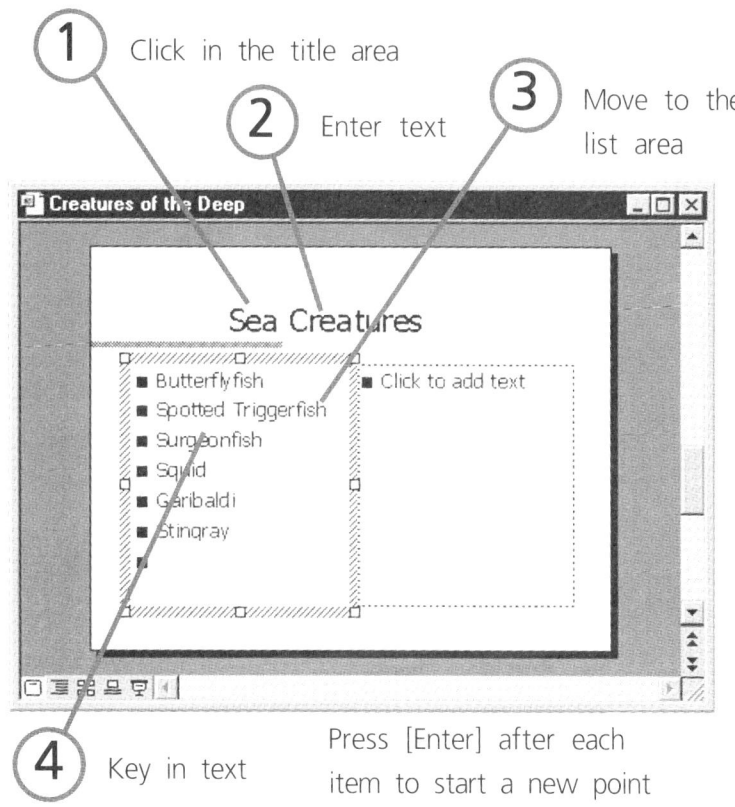

① Click in the title area

② Enter text

③ Move to the list area

④ Key in text

Press [Enter] after each item to start a new point

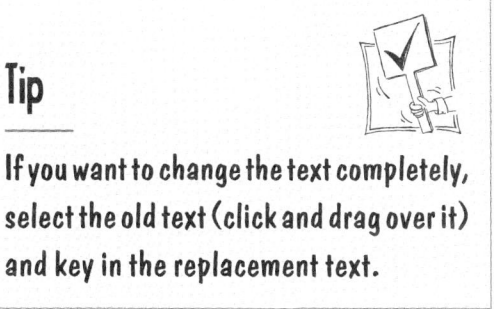

Tip

If you want to change the text completely, select the old text (click and drag over it) and key in the replacement text.

Take note

Use the Promote ⬅ and Demote ➡ tools to structure the text on your slide.

47

Formatting your text

So far, we've accepted the font formats attributed to our text by PowerPoint. You can of course change these at any time using the formatting toolbar.

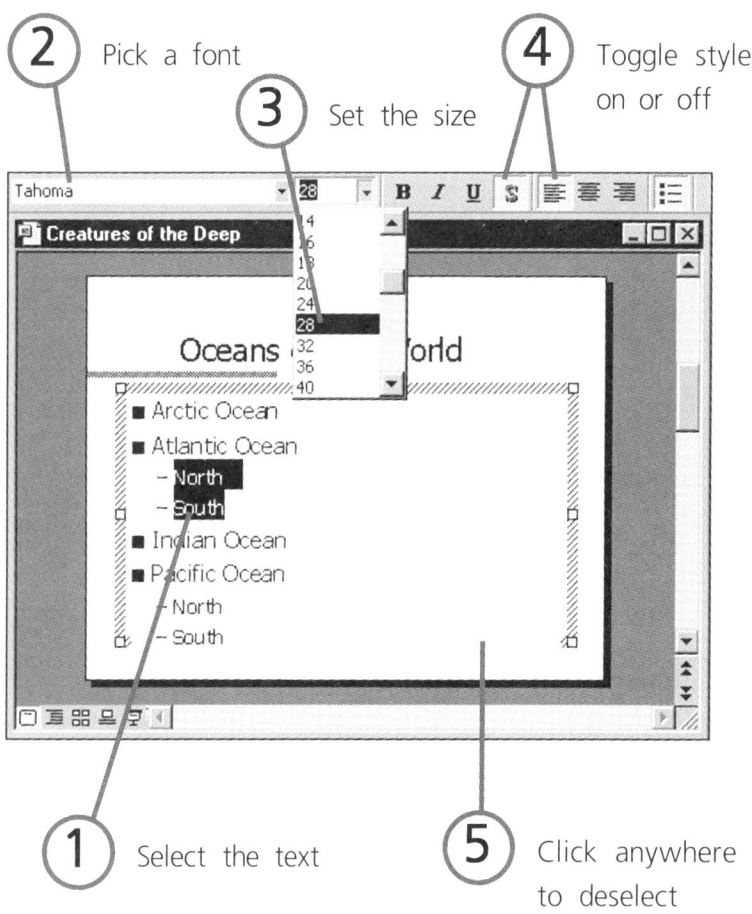

② Pick a font

③ Set the size

④ Toggle styles on or off

① Select the text

⑤ Click anywhere to deselect

Basic steps

❑ To change the font name, size or style

1 Select the text you want to format.

2 Drop down the **Font** list and choose one.

or

3 Drop down the **Font size** list and choose one.

or

4 Click the **Bold**, **Italic**, **Underline** or **Shadow** tools to switch the format on and off.

5 Deselect the text.

Keyboard shortcuts

[Ctrl]-[B] Bold, [Ctrl]-[I] Italics, [Ctrl]-[U] Underline

These all toggle the style on and off

Tip

You can change the size of selected text by clicking $\boxed{A}$ to increase or $\boxed{A}$ to decrease it to the next size in the Font Size list.

Basic steps

❑ **To change the colour**

1 Select the text

2 Choose **Font** from the **Format** menu.

3 Select a colour from the colour field (or click **More Colors...** if you want a larger choice).

4 Click [OK].

5 Deselect the text.

Take note

You can control all aspects of the text's appearance from the Font dialog box.

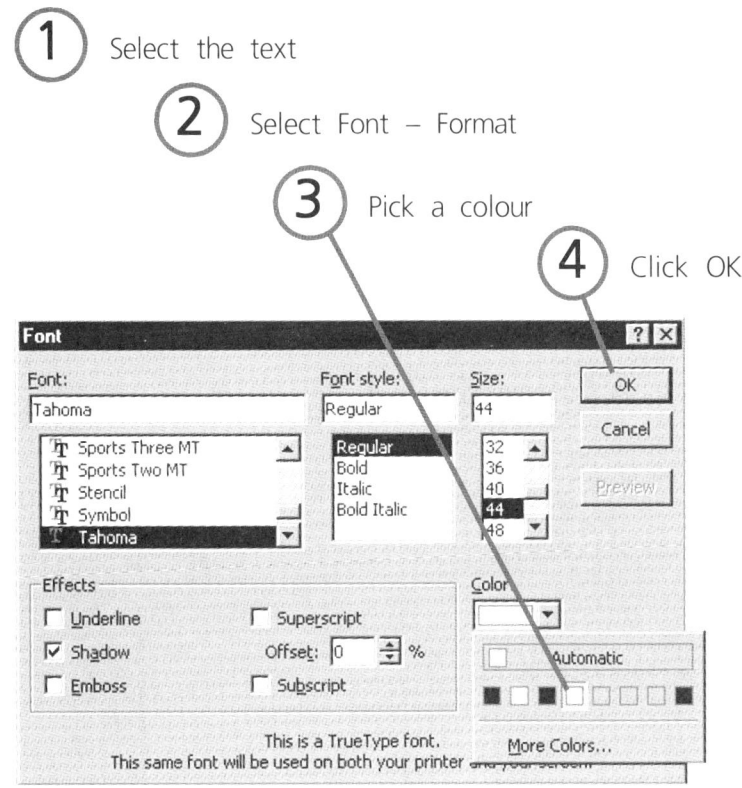

① Select the text

② Select Font – Format

③ Pick a colour

④ Click OK

The Formatting toolbar

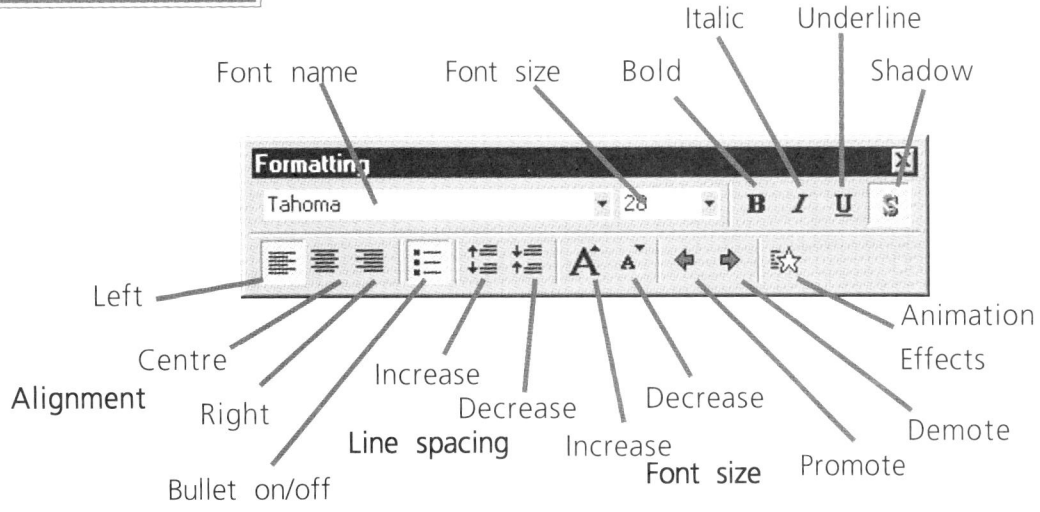

Alignment

In presentations, text is usally aligned to the left or centre. There are tools for both of these and for right alignment on the Formatting toolbar. If you want text to be justified (making the text meet both left and right margins), there is an option on the Format – Alignment menu.

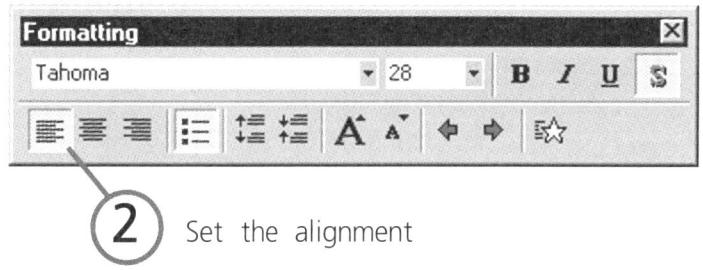

② Set the alignment

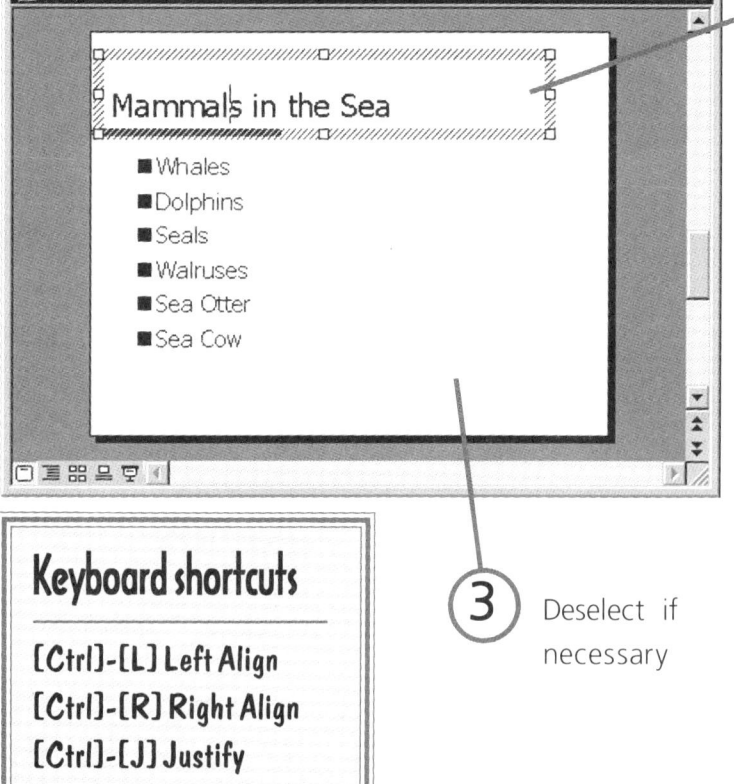

① Select the paragraph

③ Deselect if necessary

❑ **To align text**

1 Select the text you want to format.

2 Click the Left 📄, Center 📄 or Right 📄 Alignment tool.

3 If you have selected multiple paragraphs or several characters, deselect the text.

Take note

A paragraph is selected if the insertion point is within it, or at least part of it is highlighted – you don't need to select all the characters.

Keyboard shortcuts

[Ctrl]-[L] Left Align
[Ctrl]-[R] Right Align
[Ctrl]-[J] Justify
[Ctrl]-[E] Centre

Basic steps

Bullets

❑ Choosing a bullet

1 Select the point(s).

2 Open the **Format** menu and choose **Bullet**.

3 Choose a character set.

4 Select the character you want to use.

5 Set the colour and size.

6 Click [OK] to apply your changes to the slide.

In most slide layouts the text objects are formatted to display bullets at each point. The bullets can be switched off (and on again) by clicking ▤.

● If you do not like the bullets set by PowerPoint, you can choose your own.

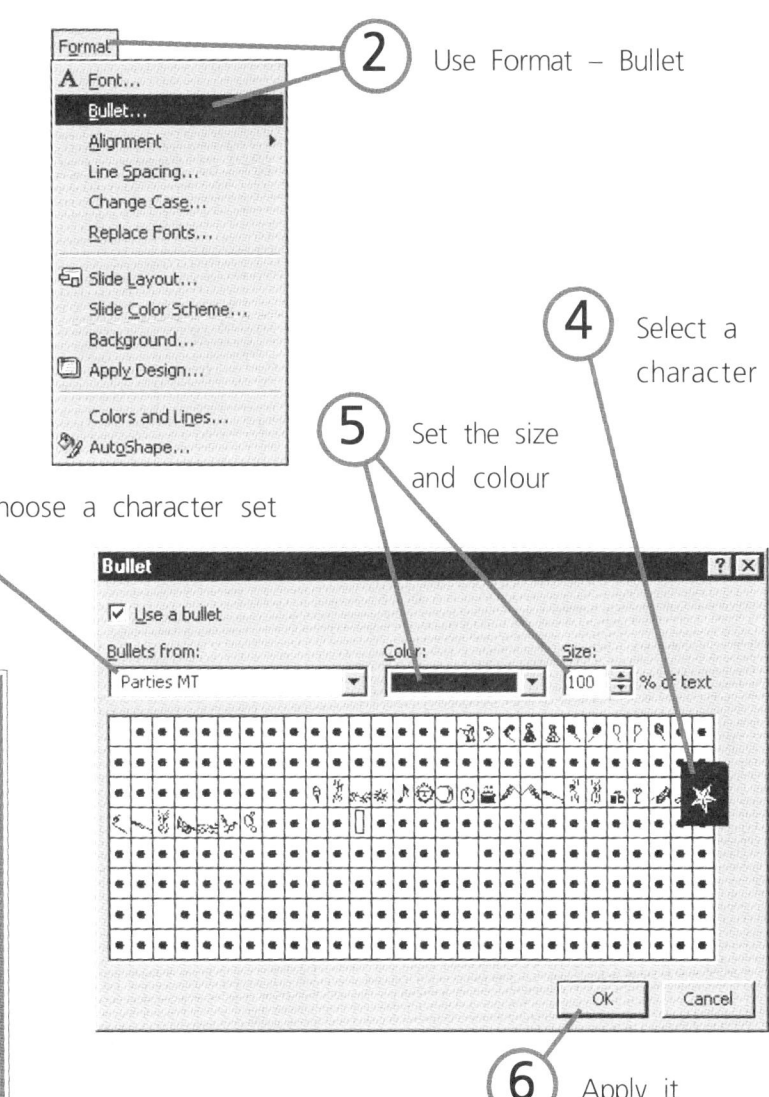

② Use Format – Bullet

③ Choose a character set

④ Select a character

⑤ Set the size and colour

⑥ Apply it

Tip

Don't change the text formatting on every slide. If you overdo things you will give your presentation an inconsistent look.

Changing a slide layout

If you decide you have chosen the wrong layout for a slide, it is easily changed from Slide view.

① View the slide

② Click the Slide Layout tool

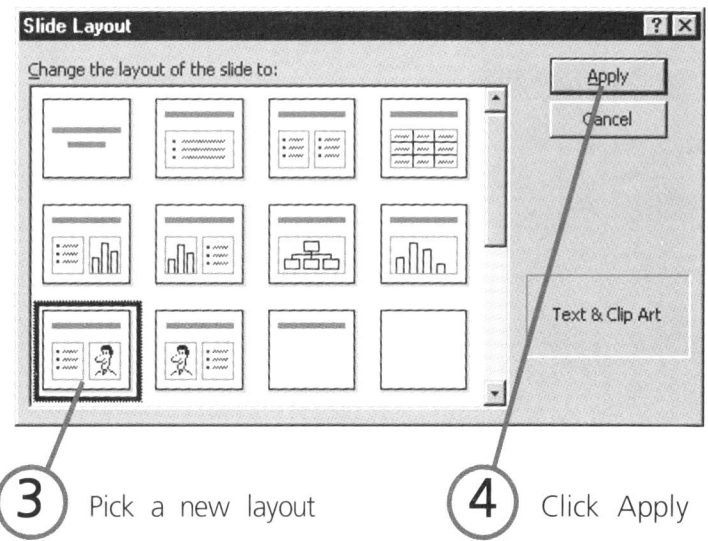

③ Pick a new layout

④ Click Apply

Take note

We look at inserting clip art in Chapter 8.

The new layout

Tip

Increase ⬆ or decrease ⬇ the paragraph spacing to get your text evenly distributed on your slide.

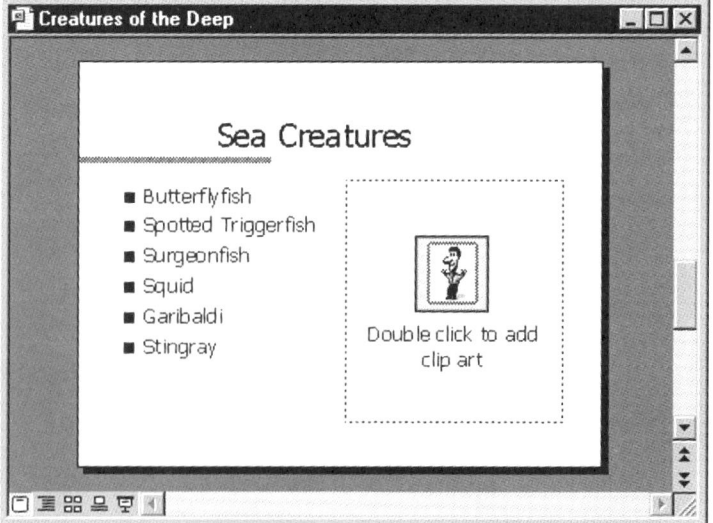

Basic steps

1 Double click the template name field on the Status bar.

or

2 Click 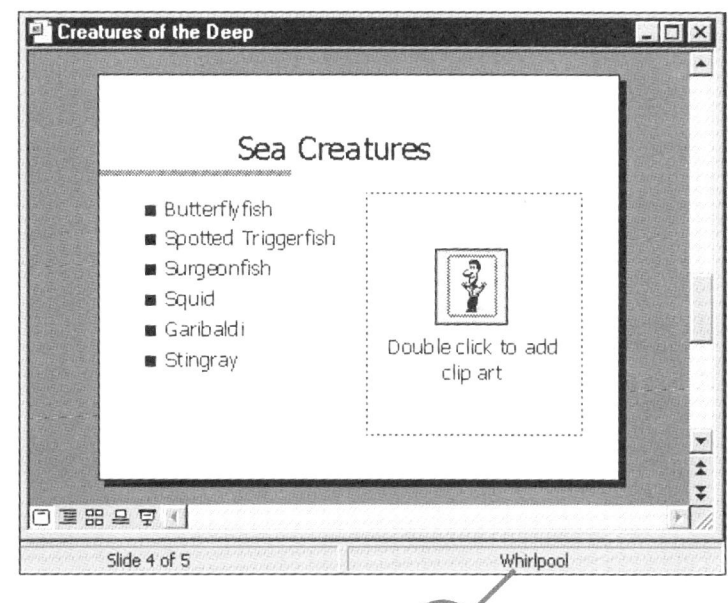 the **Apply Design Template** tool.

3 Change the folder if necessary.

4 Select the template you want to use.

5 Click [Apply].

You can change your presentation template at any time. The template determines the design elements of your presentation - colour, fonts, alignment of text, etc.

3 Change folders if required

4 Select a new template

1 Double click the template name

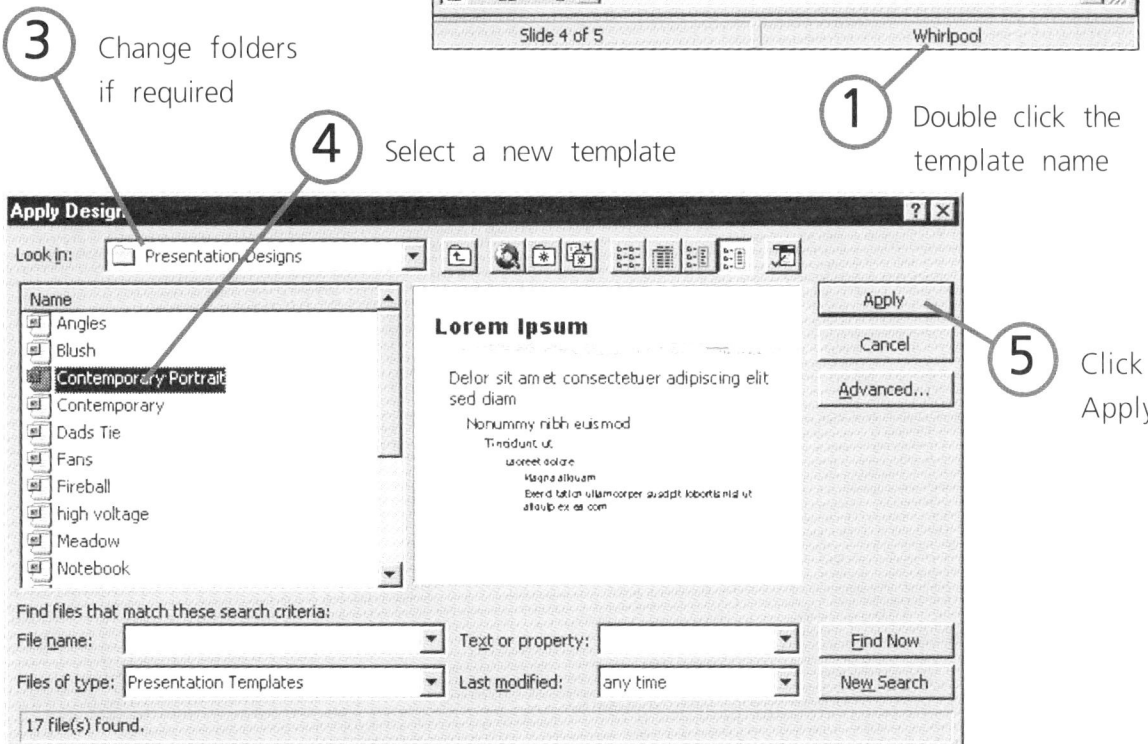

5 Click Apply

Background styles

When you select a template for your presentation, the slide background colour and shading is picked up from the options set in thc template. You can easily change the colour and shading options while still retaining the other design elements of the template.

If your presentation were in sections, e.g. on individual departments, or regional figures, you could set a different background colour for each section of your presentation.

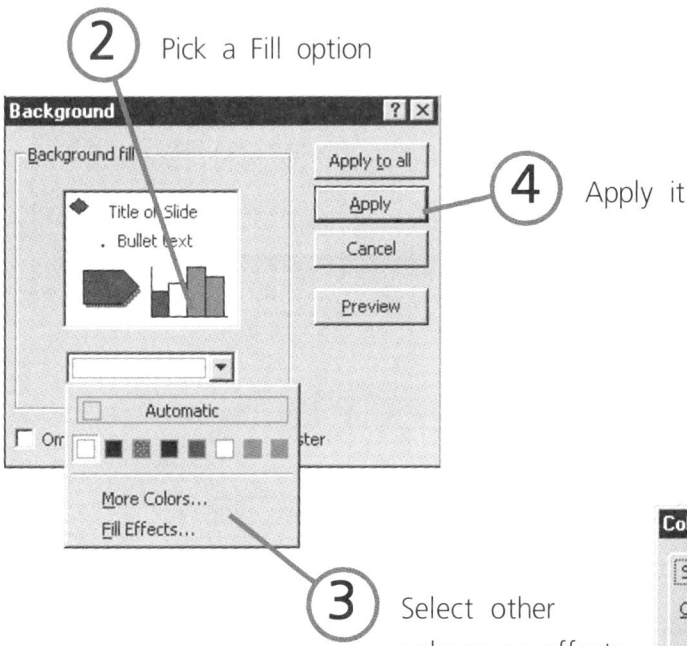

Pick a Fill option

④ Apply it

③ Select other colours or effects

(page 56)

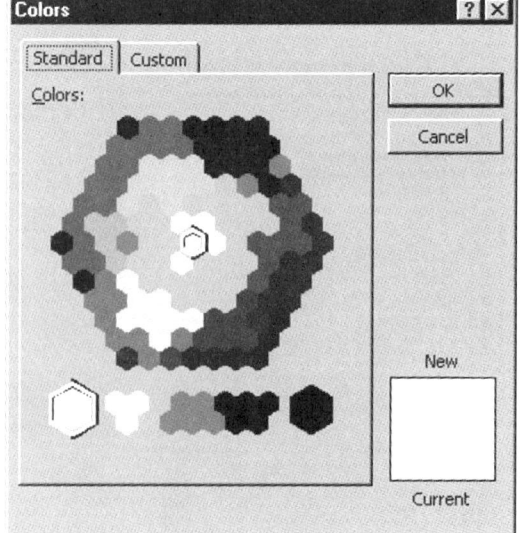

1 From the **Format** menu choose **Background**.

2 Select a **Background Fill** option from the list.

3 Click **More Colours…** and/or **Fill Effects**, if required, and select from the dialog boxes.

4 Click [Apply] to apply it to the selected slide.

or

[Preview] to see the effect.

[Apply to all] to apply it to all slides.

[Cancel] if you don't like the effect.

And yet more options.....

Experiment with the various dialog boxes to see what effects are available.

Specify your own shading (1 or 2 colours) or choose from the Preset Colours

Try one or the Textured fill effects

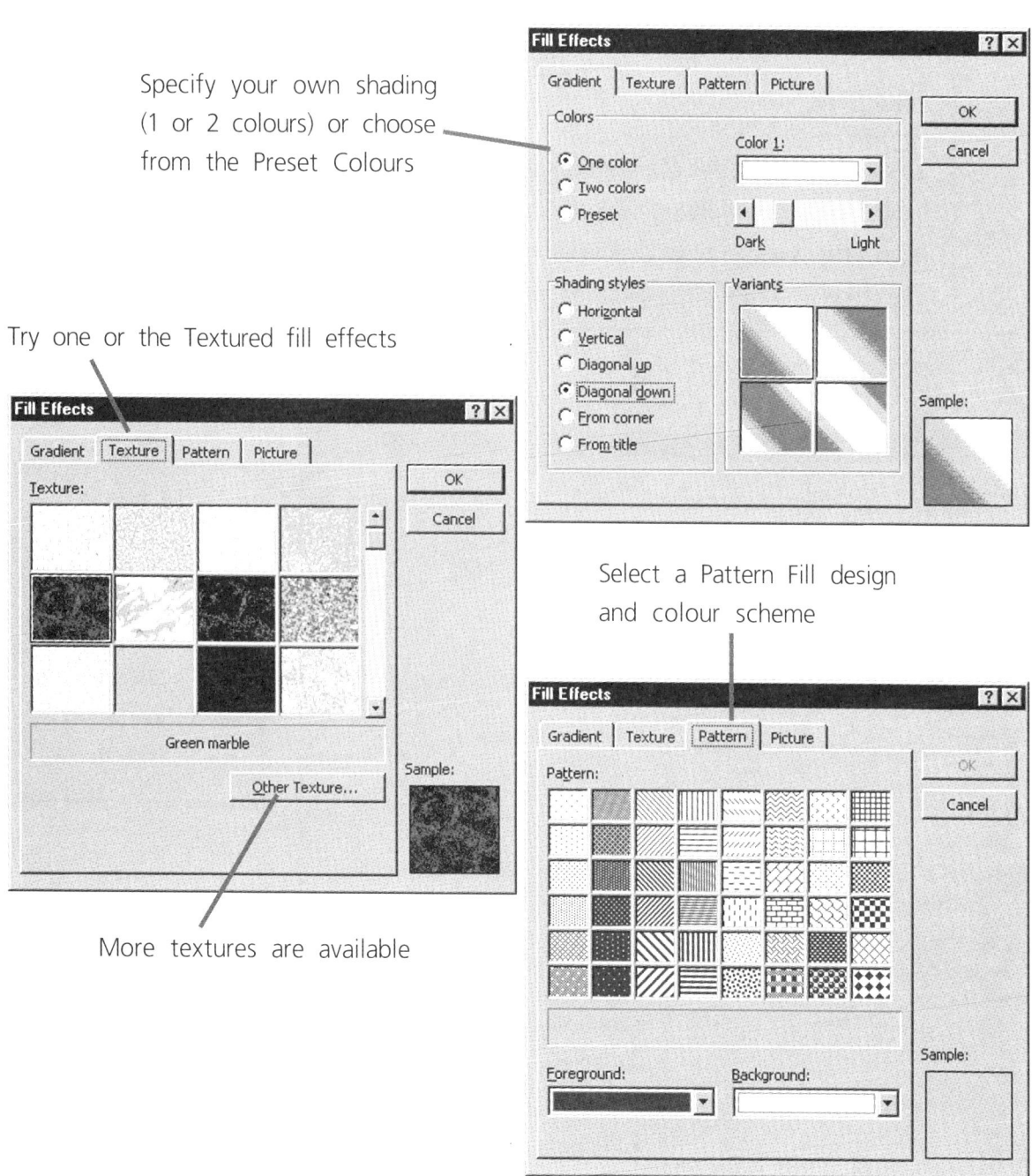

More textures are available

Select a Pattern Fill design and colour scheme

Rearranging your slides

If you need to rearrange the order your slides are in, go into Slide Sorter view.

Take note

To select several slides at once, click the first, then hold [Shift] down while you click each of the others. If you select a wrong slide, click again to deselect it. The selected set can all be moved together.

1 Click  the **Slide Sorter view** tool to go into Slide Sorter view.

2 Click on the slide you want to move.

3 Drag and drop the selected slide into its new position – the dimmed vertical line shows where it will go.

② Select the slide   ③ Drag and drop into new position

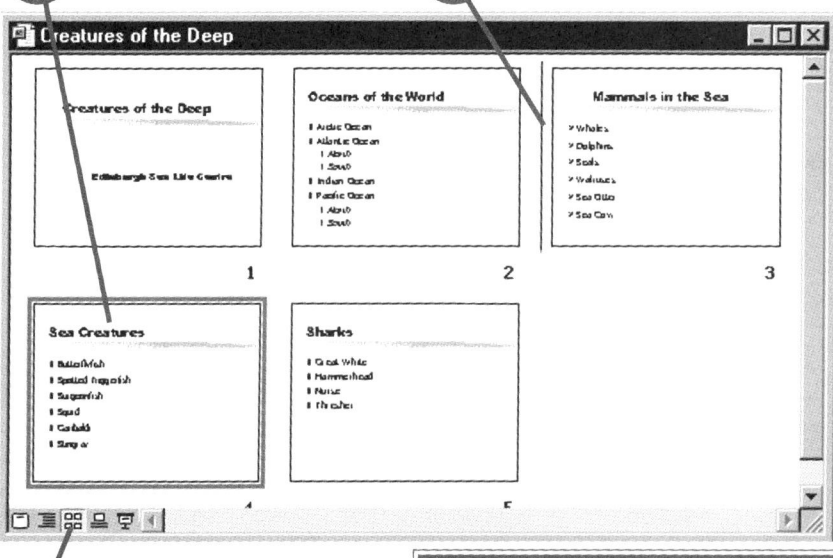

① Click Slide Sorter view

Tip

You can also move your slides around in Outline view – see Section 4.

Take note

To delete a slide in Slide Sorter view, select it and press [Delete]. To delete in Slide or Notes Page view, display the slide then choose Delete Slide from the Edit menu.

Basic steps

1 Click 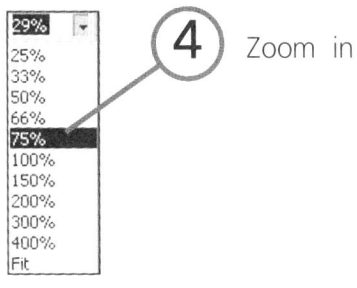 to go into **Notes Pages View**.

2 Locate the slide you want to make notes for.

3 Click in the notes area of the screen.

4 Enlarge the view of the notes area using the Zoom tool on the Standard toolbar – try 75%.

5 Key in your notes.

To help you through your presentation, you'll find things a lot easier if you have some notes to accompany your slides. You can add notes in Notes Pages view. The notes pages consist of a copy of the slide plus any notes you type in. The notes pages can be printed out so you can refer to them as you give your presentation (see Chapter 11).

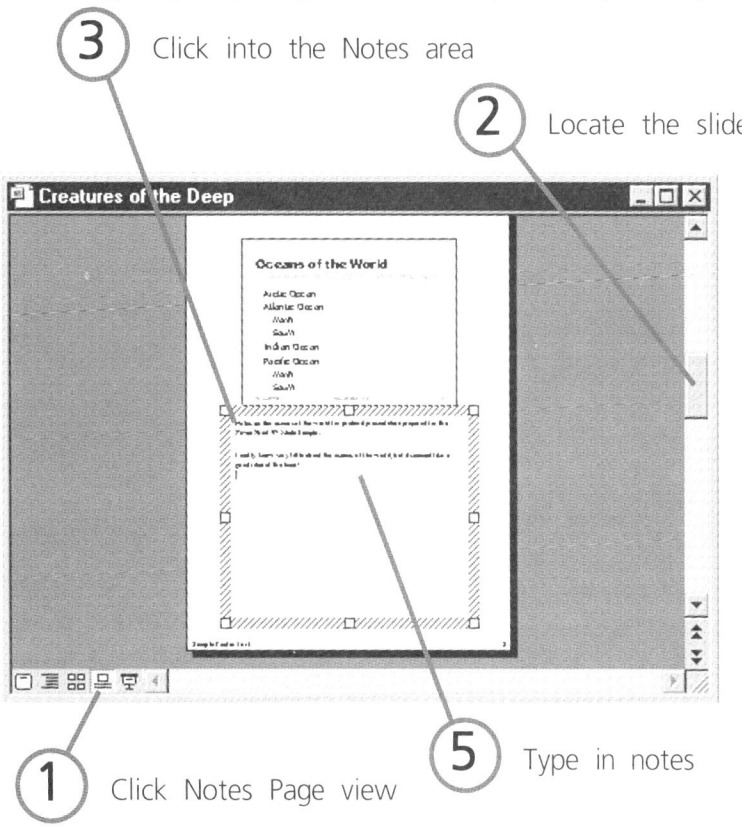

③ Click into the Notes area

② Locate the slide

⑤ Type in notes

① Click Notes Page view

④ Zoom in

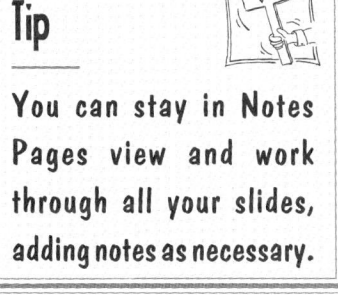

Headers & footers

If you want to add slide numbers, the date, time or any other standard text at the top or bottom of slides, notes or handouts, use the Header and Footer command.

① Open the View menu

② Choose Header and Footer...

Set Automatic
or
Fixed date

③ Select a tab

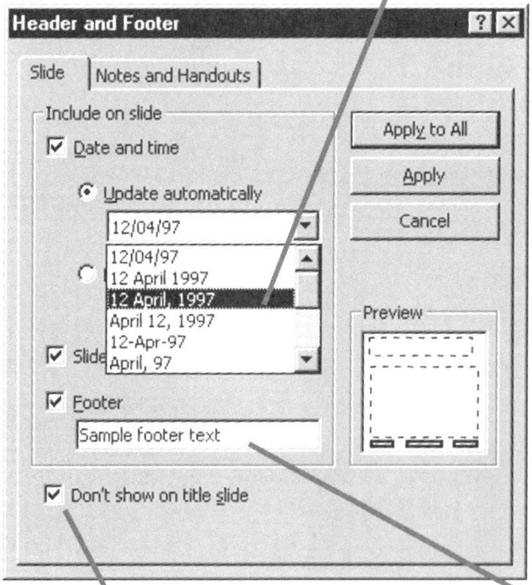

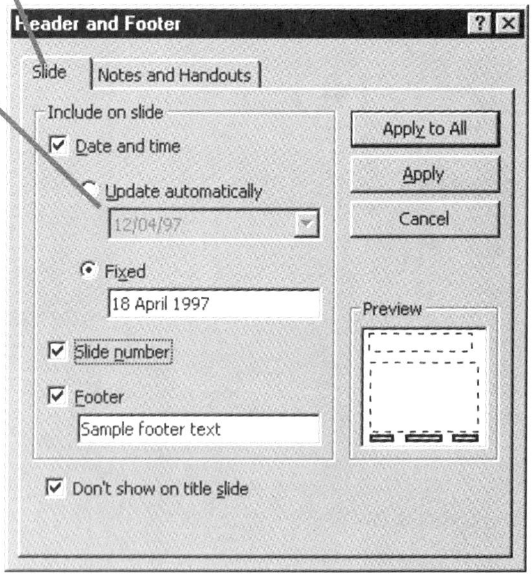

Select to leave items off title slide   Footer wanted?

④ Set options as required

Basic steps

1 Open the **View** menu.

2 Choose **Header and Footer...**

3 Select the appropriate tab – **Slides** or **Notes and Handouts**.

4 Tick the items you want to appear, giving details as needed.

5 Click [Apply] or [Apply to all].

58

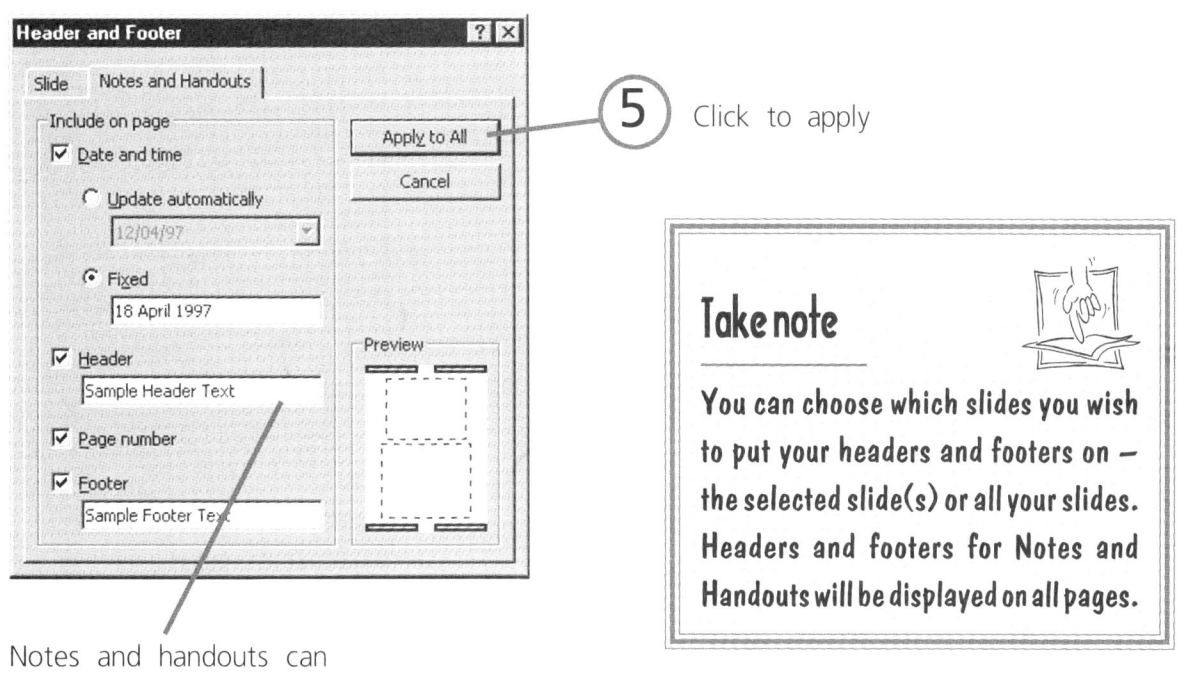

⑤ Click to apply

Take note

You can choose which slides you wish to put your headers and footers on — the selected slide(s) or all your slides. Headers and footers for Notes and Handouts will be displayed on all pages.

Notes and handouts can also have a Header

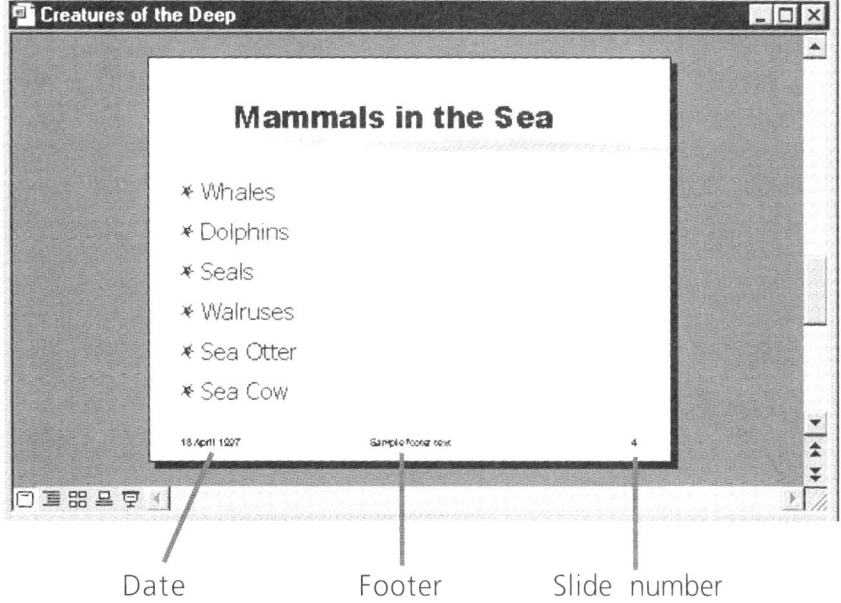

Date   Footer   Slide number

Summary

❏ You can **add text**, **clip art**, **organisation charts**, **tables**, **graphs**, etc. in Slide view.

❏ **New slides** can be added anywhere in a presentation using the New Slide tool on the Standard toolbar.

❏ Text for the slide title, or for the points you wish to list, is keyed into **placeholders** on the slide.

❏ The points listed on a slide usually have **bullets** beside them. You can switch these off, or choose a different bullet from the available character sets.

❏ To change the layout of a slide, click the **Slide Layout** tool on the Standard toolbar then choose the layout you want from the dialog box.

❏ You can delete a slide by choosing **Delete Slide** from the Edit menu.

❏ To change the presentation Template, double click the **Template name field** on the status bar, then select an alternative Template from the list.

❏ You can easily change the background formatting for your slide.

❏ To rearrange your slides go into **Slide Sorter view,** then click and drag your slides to their new positions.

❏ You can add notes to your slides in **Notes Pages view.**

❏ **Headers** and **footers** can be switched on and off from the Header and Footer dialog box.

6 Drawing and WordArt

Selecting objects

So far, we have dealt with text objects – slide headings and points listed for discussion on the slides.

In this section we are going to consider how the tools on the Drawing toolbar can be used to customise and add interest to your slides. You must be in Slide view for this.

Select Objects tool

The Select Objects tool is used to select objects on your slide. Once an object has been selected, you can move it, resize it, delete it (and lots of other things as we'll soon see).

The Select Objects tool on the Drawing toolbar is always selected unless you pick another tool from the toolbar.

❏ **To select a text object**

1 Position the mouse pointer over any text within the placeholder area and click.

Note the handles that appear at the corners and along the edges of the selected object.

❏ **To select other objects**

2 Click anywhere inside the object placeholder.

❏ **To deselect an object**

3 Click anywhere outside the selected object (click inside or outside a text object).

The Drawing toolbar

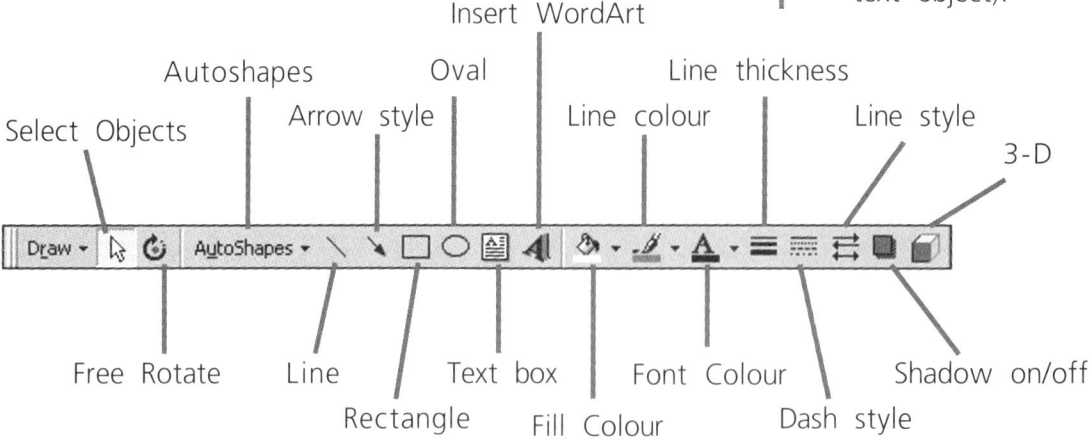

❏ Moving

Point to the *border* of a text object, or anywhere *within* any other type of object (not a handle) and drag it to its new position.

❏ Resizing

Point to one of the **handles** (note the mouse pointer) and drag it until the object is the required size.

❏ Deleting a text object

Select the text object, click the border once, then press [**Delete**].

❏ Deleting other objects
Select, then press [Delete].

Take note

If you delete an object by mistake, click the Undo tool on the Standard toolbar.

1 Click in the text to get the border

Drag the border to move

Drag a handle to resize

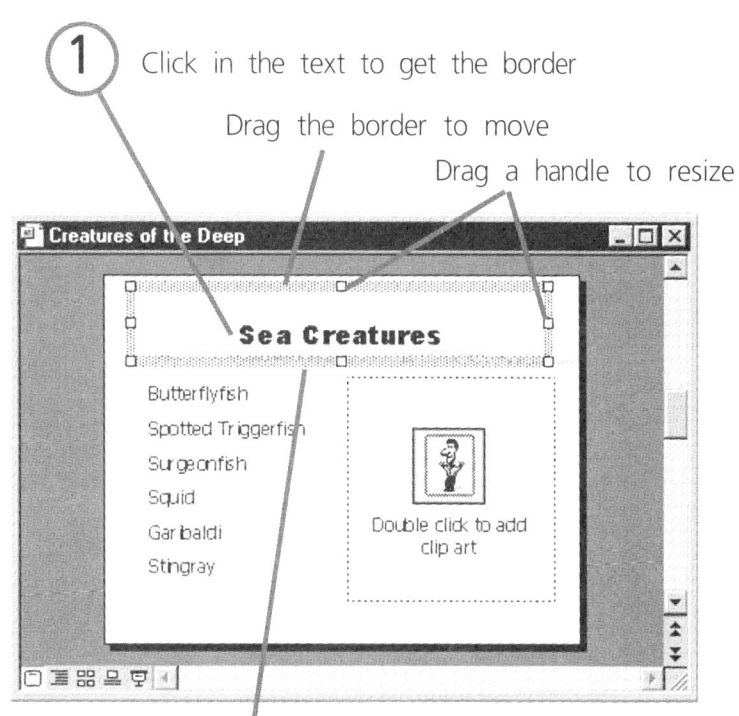

Click on the border then press [Delete] to delete the whole text box

2 Click in the area to select   3 Click outside to deselect

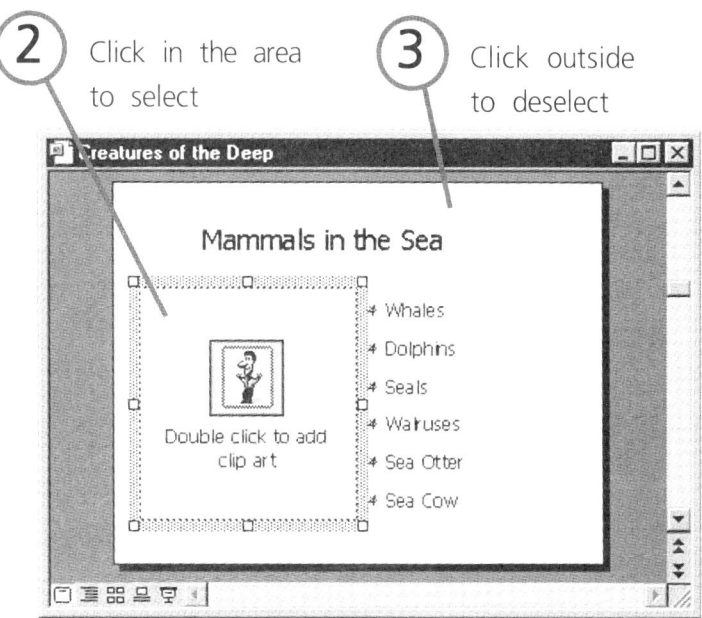

Text box tool

You can use the Text box tool to enter text **anywhere** on your slide (not necessarily within an existing text placeholder).

Basic steps

1 Select  the **Text box** tool.

2 Click anywhere on your slide to position the insertion point.

3 Key in the text.

4 Format the text as required.

❑ The text object you have created can be selected, moved, resized and deleted (see page 63).

 Position the insertion point

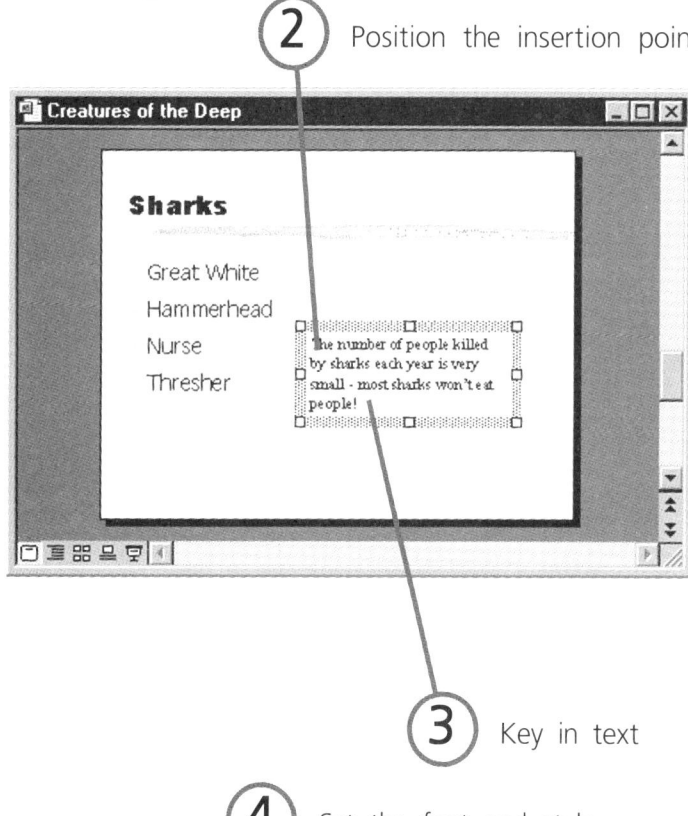

Creatures of the Deep

Sharks

Great White
Hammerhead
Nurse
Thresher

The number of people killed by sharks each year is very small - most sharks won't eat people!

3 Key in text

4 Set the font and style

Take note

You can format the text using any of the text formatting options — bold, size, font style, italics, underline etc.

Take note

Text objects can be placed within an AutoShape to add emphasis (see page 66) or rotated to create interesting effects on your slides (see page 67).

Basic steps

❏ **Line based tools**

1 Select a tool – line, arrow, rectangle or oval \\ ↖ □ ○ .

2 Click to set the start.

3 Drag to draw a shape.

❏ **Different effects**

4 Select the object.

Change the Fill or Line colour 🪣 ▾ 🖌 ▾ .

Set the line, dash or arrow style ≡ ≡ ⇄ .

Add a shadow or 3-D effect ▣ ◩ .

5 Deselect the object.

Tip

To select a drawing object, click anywhere within it.

Drawing tools

The line, arrow, rectangle and oval tools all work in a similar way. You can customise a shape in many ways – give it a shadow, or 3-D effect, change the line colour and thickness, or experiment with fill colours and patterns. Experiment with the other tools to change the appearance of your objects.

Oval with shadow   3-D rectangle

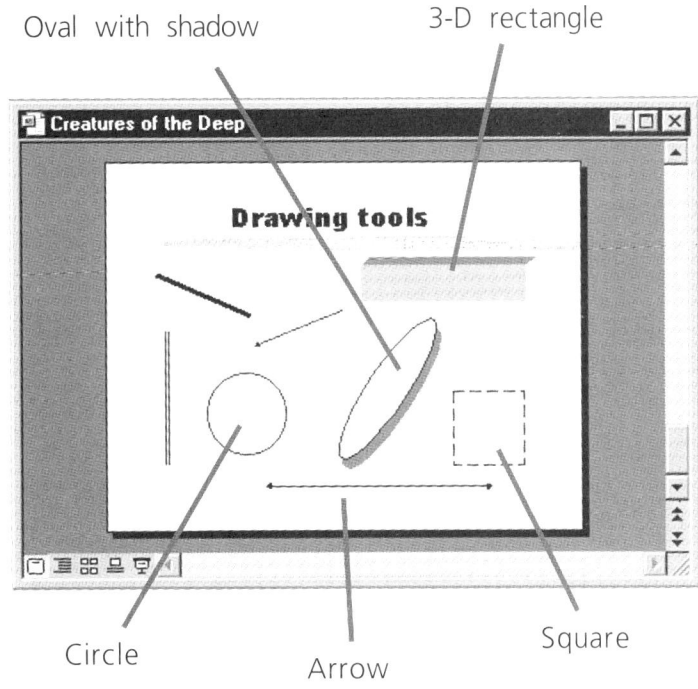

Circle   Arrow   Square

Take note

If you need to draw several lines, arrows, rectangles or ovals, you can 'lock' the desired tool on. Double click a tool to lock it on. Draw as many shapes as you need. Select any other tool, or press [Esc], to unlock it.

AutoShapes

You may find the shape you need under AutoShapes. If you want stars, triangles, arrows etc on your slide you'll find lots to choose from. AutoShapes can be drawn and formatted in the same way as the basic drawing shapes.

● The Freeform and Curve AutoShapes in the Lines category don't quite follow the basic 'click and drag' principle adopted by the other drawing tools.

Experiment with the various options.

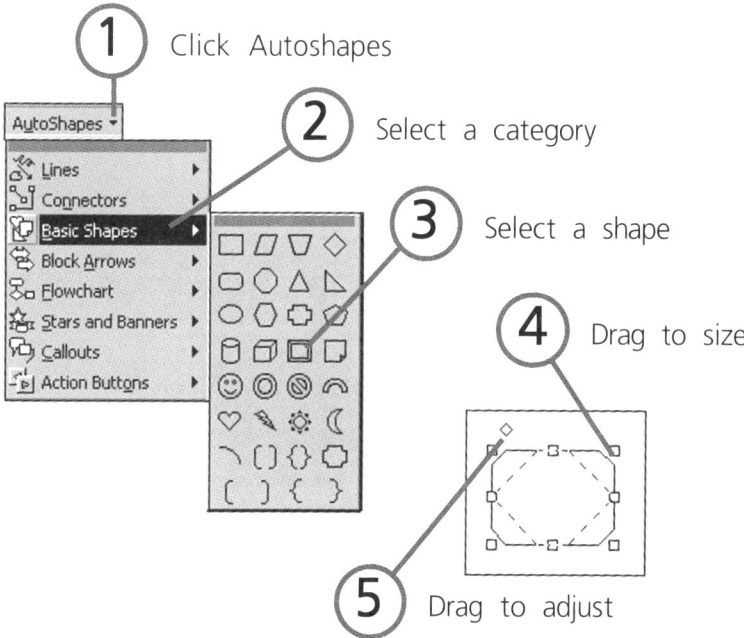

Click Autoshapes

Select a category

Select a shape

Drag to size

Drag to adjust

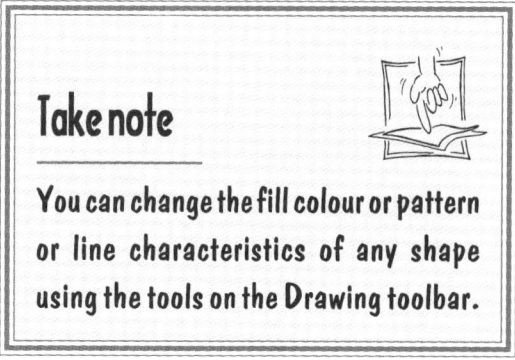

Take note

You can change the fill colour or pattern or line characteristics of any shape using the tools on the Drawing toolbar.

Basic steps

1 Click the **AutoShapes** tool to display the categories available.

2 Select a category.

3 Choose a shape.

4 Click and drag to draw.

5 Drag the ◇ handle to adjust the shape.

❑ **Freeform**

6 Click and drag (note the pencil shaped pointer) to draw lines freehand.

Or, to get a straight line

7 Click at the start, then click again at the end.

❑ **Curve**

8 Click to set the start and click where you want each curve to be.

9 Press **[Esc]** when done to switch the tool off.

Take note

The Action Buttons are discussed in Chapter 12.

66

Basic steps

1 Select the object you wish to rotate or flip.

2 Choose **Rotate or Flip** from the **Draw** menu.

3 Select the option required from the submenu.

4 With the **Free Rotate** tool, drag a rotate handle to turn the shape.

Take note

The Rotate or Flip submenu can be dragged to 'float' on your screen. Click and drag its title bar. Any submenu with a title bar can become a floating menu.

Rotate or Flip

Once an object has been drawn, you can flip it over horizontally or vertically, or rotate it right or left to get the effect you want.

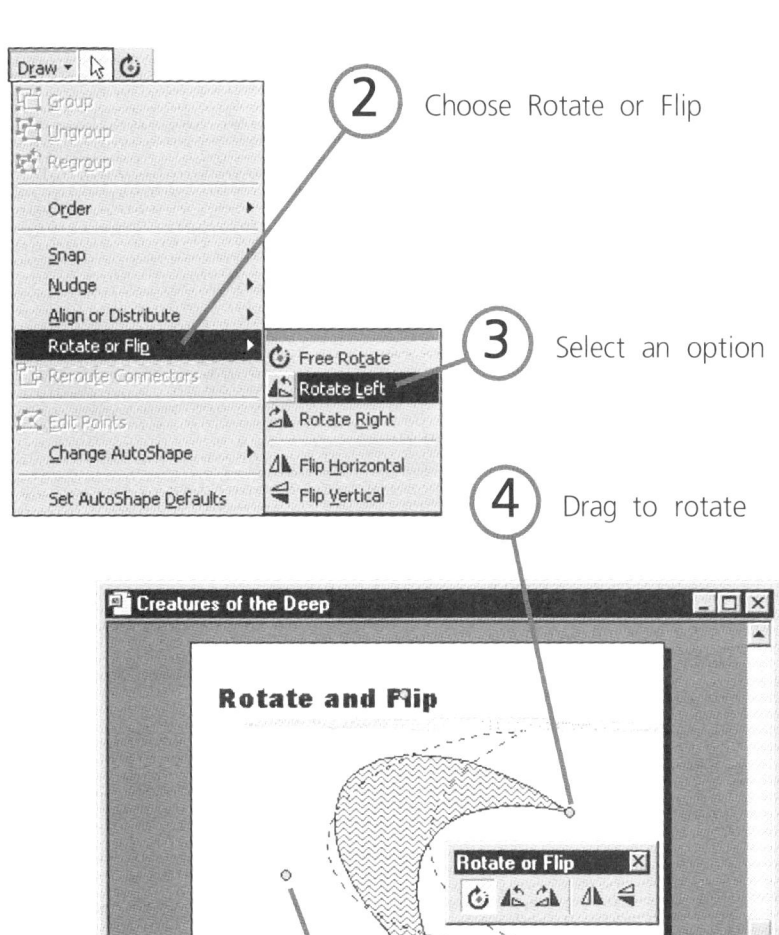

② Choose Rotate or Flip

③ Select an option

④ Drag to rotate

Rotate handles

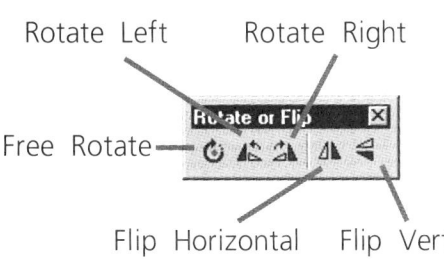

Rotate Left   Rotate Right

Free Rotate

Flip Horizontal   Flip Vertical

Changing the order

When you draw objects onto your slides, they lie in layers relative to the order in which they are drawn. The first object is on the bottom layer, the next one on a layer above the first one and so on.

Using this layering principle, you can create complex drawings by overlapping objects one on top of another.

If you need to rearrange the layering of your objects, you can do so using the Bring Forward and Send Backward commands.

1 Select the object you wish to **Bring Forward** or **Send Backward**.

2 Open the **Draw** menu.

3 Select **Order**.

4 Choose the option required.

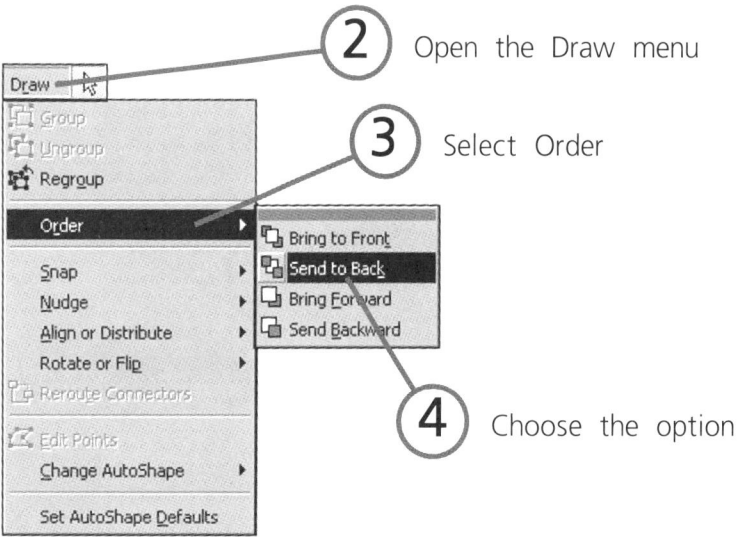

Open the Draw menu

Select Order

Choose the option

Take note

Bring to Front and Send to Back move the selected object to the top or bottom of the pile of objects. Bring Forward and Send Backward move the selected object through the pile one layer at a time.

Tip

Right click on the selected object to open the Shortcut menu. Select Order from it and specify the options required.

Basic steps

1 Select the objects you want to group.

❑ Select the first object then hold **[Shift]** down when you select the other objects.

❑ To select all the objects on a slide use **[Ctrl]-[A]** or drag over them.

2 Open the **Draw** menu.

3 Select **Group**.

If you have drawn several objects to generate an image, you can group the objects together into one to make it easier to move, copy or resize the whole image.

① Select the objects

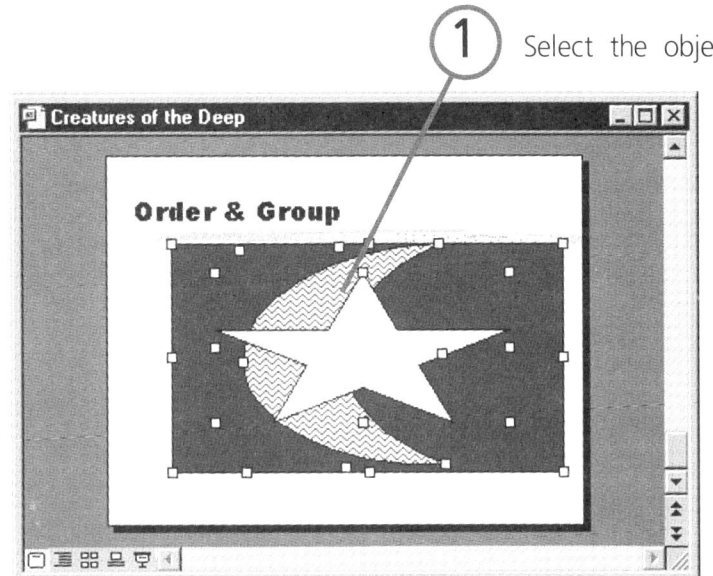

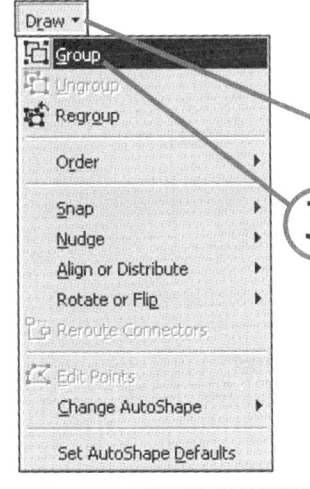

② Open the Draw menu

③ Select Group

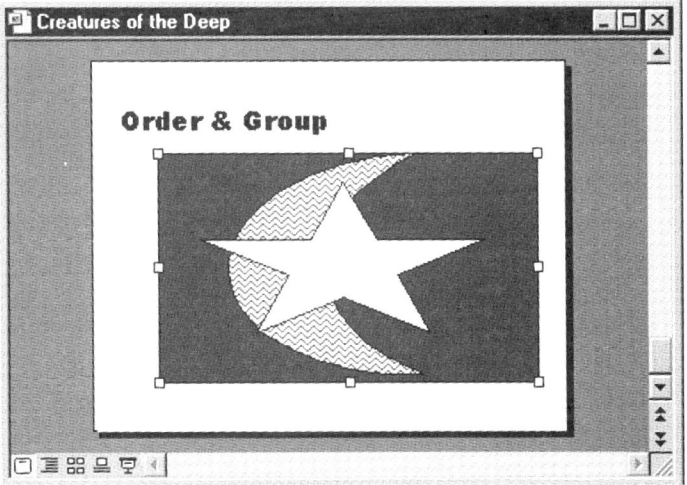

Tip

To edit a grouped object, select it and use **Draw – Ungroup** to separate it into its original objects.

WordArt

With WordArt you can create special text effects on your slides. It allows you to produce stunning title slides and real eye-catchers wherever they are needed.

Basic steps

1 Click the **Insert WordArt** tool.

2 Select a WordArt style from the **Gallery**.

3 Click [OK].

4 At the **Edit WordArt Text** dialog box, enter (and format) the text.

5 Click [OK].

6 Adjust the shape of your WordArt object as required.

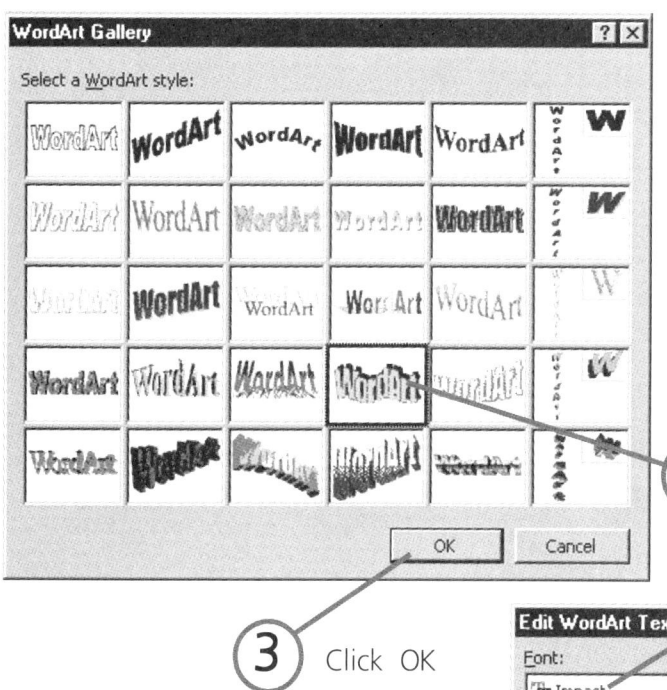

② Select a style

③ Click OK

④ Enter and format text

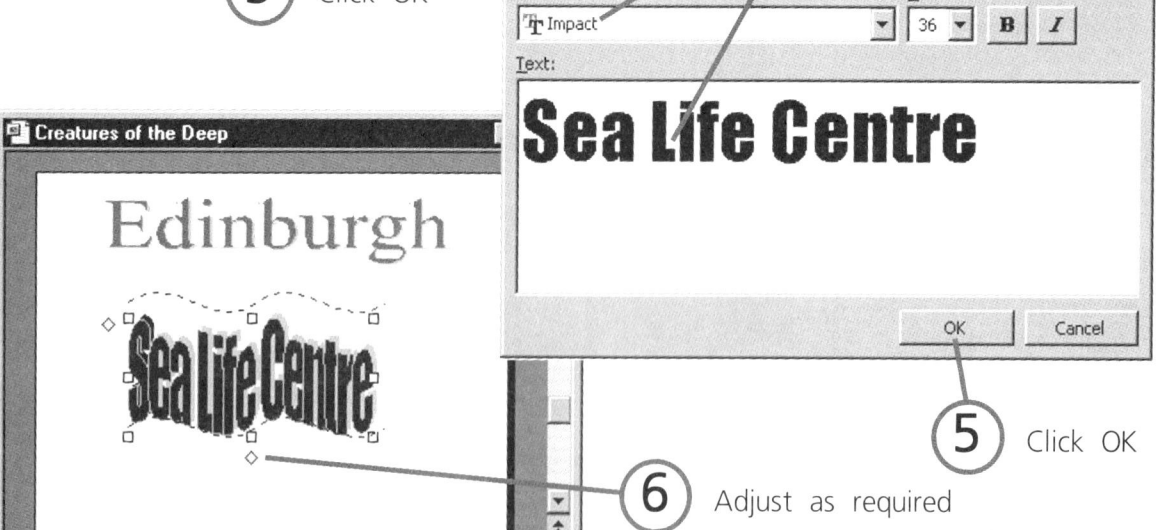

⑤ Click OK

⑥ Adjust as required

The WordArt toolbar

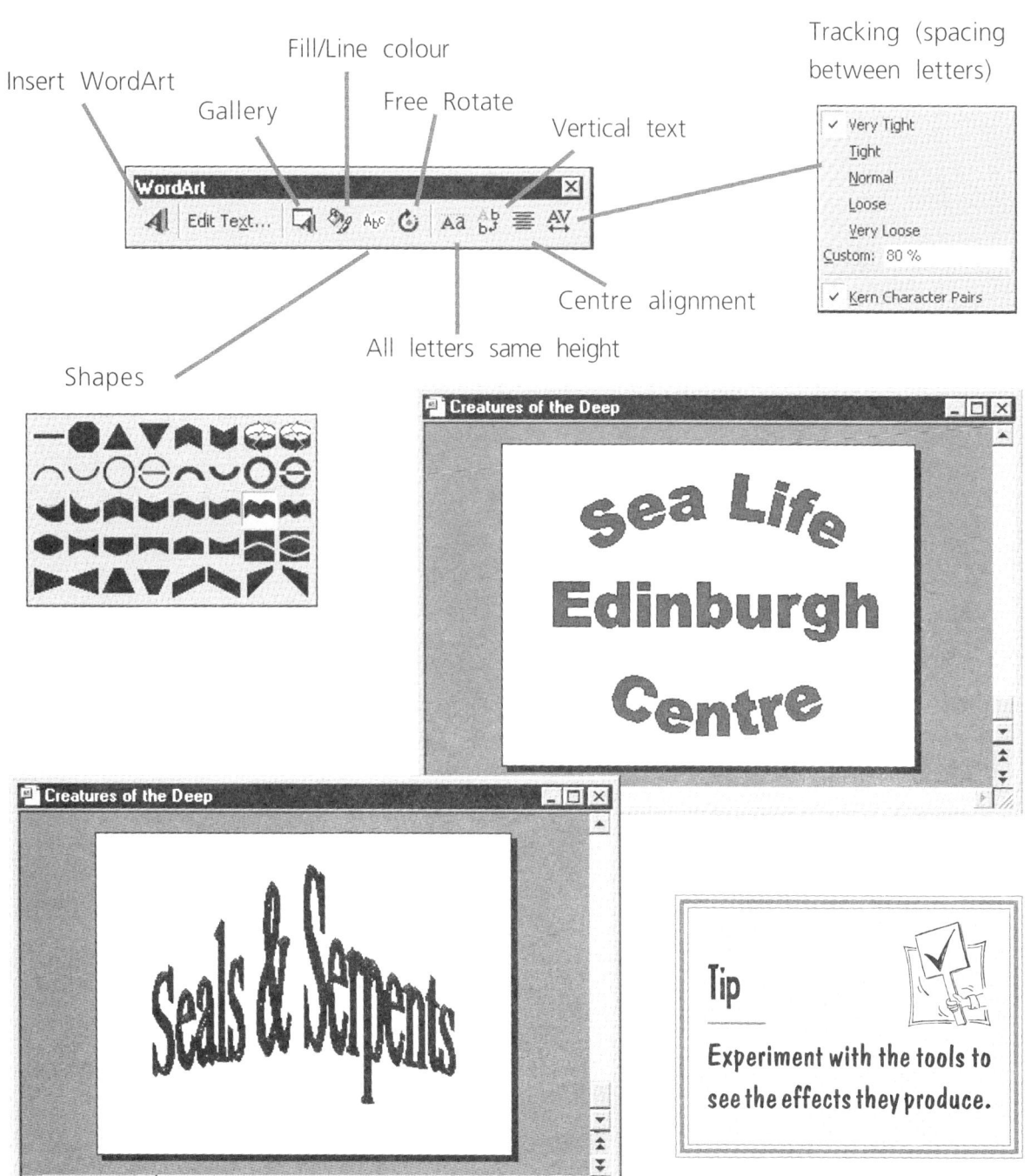

Insert WordArt

Gallery

Fill/Line colour

Free Rotate

Vertical text

Tracking (spacing between letters)

Centre alignment

All letters same height

Shapes

Summary

❏ To move, resize or delete an object, you must **select it first.**

❏ A selected object can easily be **moved, resized or deleted.**

❏ You can use the Line, Rectangle, Oval and AutoShape tools to create **drawings** on your slides.

❏ You can **add text** anywhere on your slide using the Text box tool.

❏ The **AutoShapes** toolbar contains several useful shapes to add impact to your presentations.

❏ Objects can be **rotated** using the Free Rotate and Rotate tools, or **mirrored** with the Flip tools.

❏ Drawing objects can **overlap** each other and can be layered to produce the image you require.

❏ Drawing objects can be **moved backwards and forwards** relative to each other.

❏ Many drawings consist of several objects. The objects can be '**grouped**' together to make it easier to move, resize or delete an image.

❏ **Fill colours, lines** and **shadows** are easily customised.

❏ **WordArt** gives you access to many special text effects.

7 Charts

Creating a chart

There will be times when pictures talk louder than words – and when this is the case you can use charts, organisation charts, clip art, tables, etc to help you make your point. In this section we'll look at ways you can add a chart or graph to your slide.

There are three main ways to set up your chart using Microsoft Graph 97:

● Choose a slide from the New Slide dialog box that has a chart placeholder already on it;

  or

● Choose a slide from the New Slide dialog box that has an object placeholder already on it;

  or

● Click the Insert Chart tool.

❑ Using a chart placeholder

1 Double click within the **chart** placeholder to start Microsoft Graph.

❑ From a slide with no placeholder set

1 Click the **Insert Chart** tool on the Standard toolbar

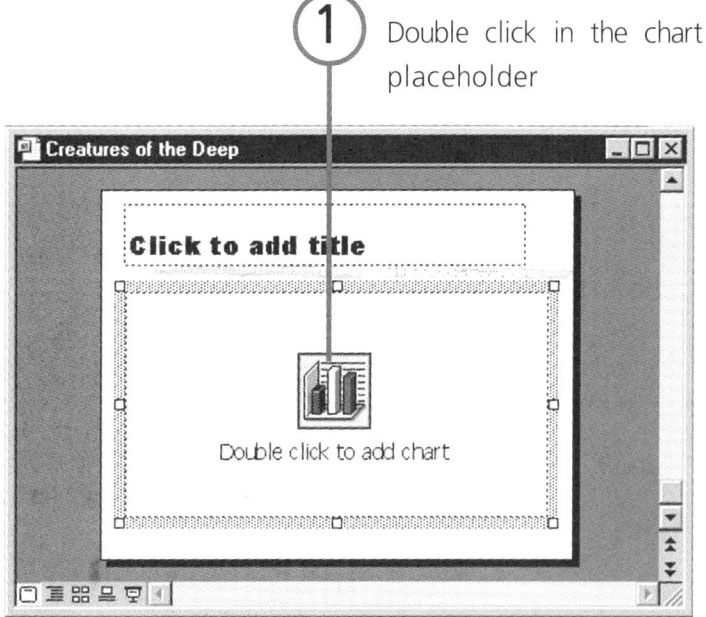

① Double click in the chart placeholder

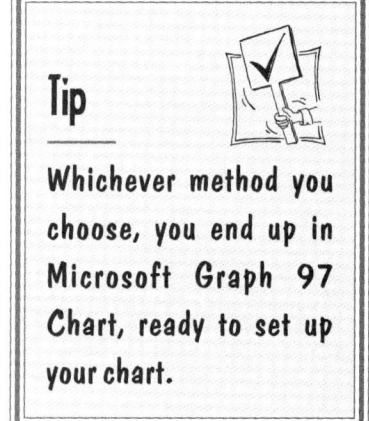

Tip

Whichever method you choose, you end up in Microsoft Graph 97 Chart, ready to set up your chart.

Basic steps

❑ Using an object placeholder

1 Double click within the **object** placeholder on your slide to open the **Insert Object** dialog box.

2 Choose **Microsoft Graph 97 Chart**.

3 Click ⬚ OK ⬚.

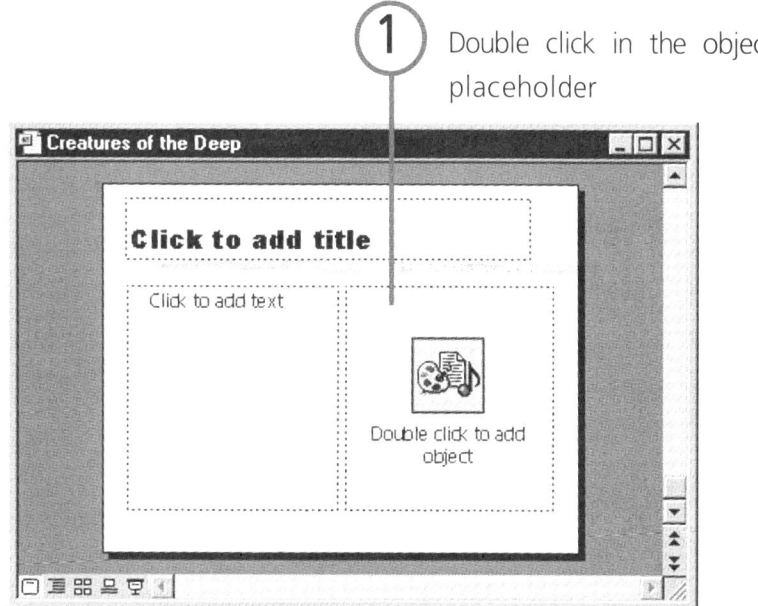

① Double click in the object placeholder

② Select Microsoft Graph 97 Chart

③ Click OK

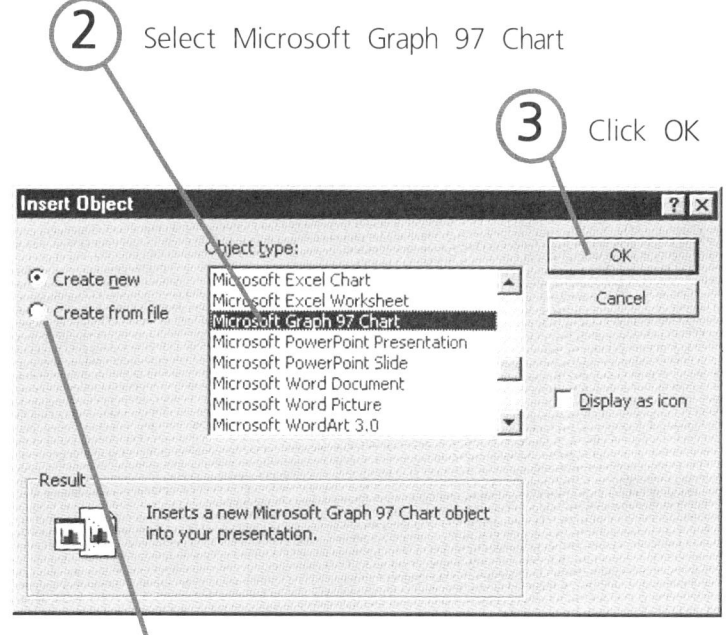

Use the file option to import a chart that you created earlier

Datasheet and toolbars

The Graph 97 environment has its own Standard and Formatting toolbars. There is also a small Datasheet window (which can be moved or resized as necessary), where you can key in the data you want to chart.

Entering your own data

You must replace the sample data in the datasheet with the data you want to chart. If you do not need to replace all the sample data, delete the cell contents that are not required – go to the cell and press [Delete].

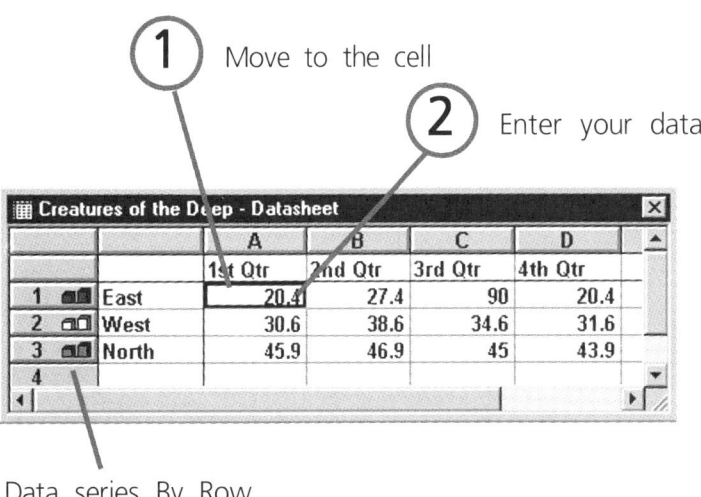

① Move to the cell

② Enter your data

Data series By Row

View/hide datasheet

Once you have keyed in your data, you can Hide the datasheet so you can see the chart clearly on your screen. If you hide your datasheet, you can easily view it again if you need to edit any data. Click  the view Datasheet tool to view or hide the Datasheet, as required.

Basic steps

1 Go to the cell into which you wish to enter your own data

2 Key in the data

3 Move to the next cell you want to work on, use any of the methods shown opposite

Take note

The Category axis has labels taken from the column or row headings in your datasheet. Use **By Row** and **By Column** on the Standard toolbar to indicate whether your data series is in rows or columns. A graphic in the row or column heading of your datasheet indicates the selected option.

The Value axis is the one your data is plotted against.

Moving around your datasheet

Tip

Don't enter too much data — the chart will be seen on a slide or overhead. If it's too detailed your audience may not fully appreciate it!

There are a number of ways to move from cell to cell within the Datasheet. Use the keys:

Arrow keys	one cell in direction of arrow
[Tab]	forward to the next cell
[Shift]-[Tab]	back to the previous cell
[Enter]	down to the next cell in a column

or

Point to the cell and click.

The cell you are in (your *current* cell) has a dark border.

Standard toolbar

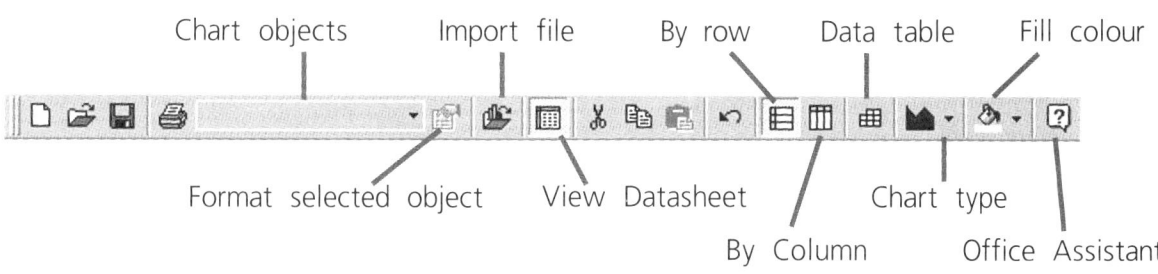

Chart objects   Import file   By row   Data table   Fill colour

Format selected object   View Datasheet   Chart type

By Column   Office Assistant

Formatting toolbar

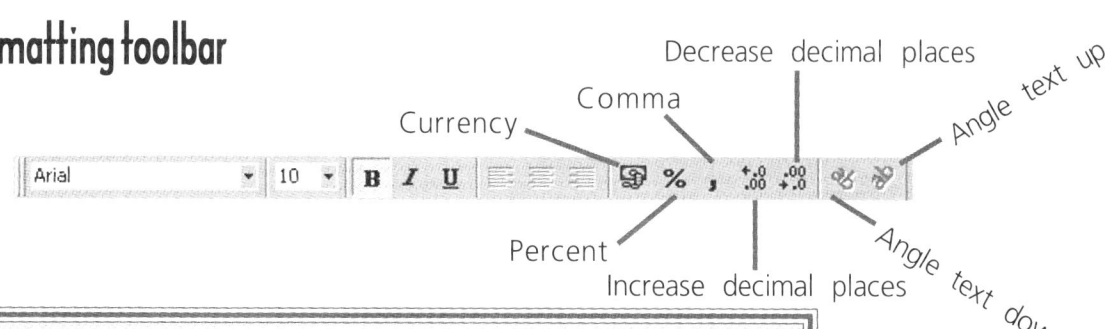

Decrease decimal places   Angle text up

Comma

Currency

Percent   Angle text down

Increase decimal places

Number formats

Numbers can be displayed Currency, Comma or Percent styles

Currency: £1,565.75   Comma: 1,565.75   Percent: 156575%

Select the cell(s), and click a style tool on the Formatting toolbar.

77

Chart type

The default chart type is a column chart. You can try out a variety of other chart types using the Chart Type tool on the Standard toolbar.

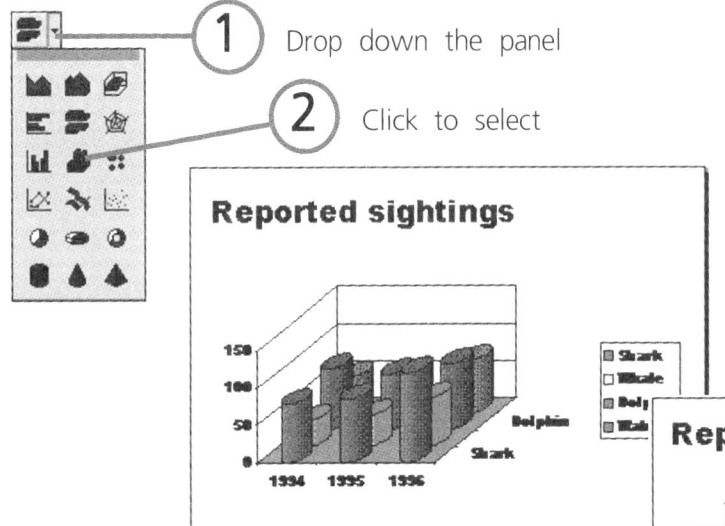

① Drop down the panel

② Click to select

Reported sightings

Vertical charts (left) are usually more effective than horizontal ones (below)

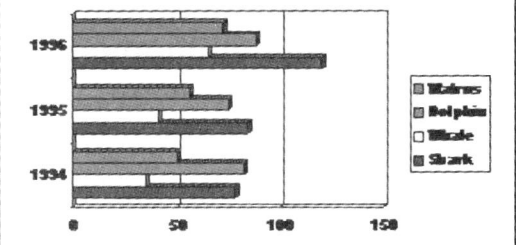

Reported sightings

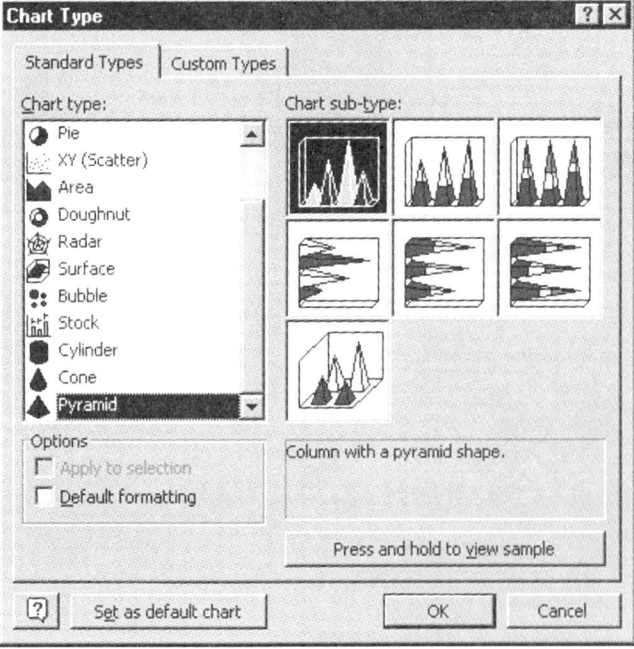

> **Tip**
>
> Open the Chart menu and choose Chart Type... You'll find lots of other options to choose from.

Basic steps

1 Display the datasheet if necessary.

2 Double click on the heading of the column or row you wish to hide.

  The data is dimmed, and is not displayed on your chart.

3 Double click the heading again to reveal the column or row.

You can customise the basic chart in a number of different ways, to add your own personal touch. Have a look through the menus to see what options are available to you.

Hiding columns

If you don't want all your data to be displayed, you can hide rows or columns as required. This is done on the datasheet.

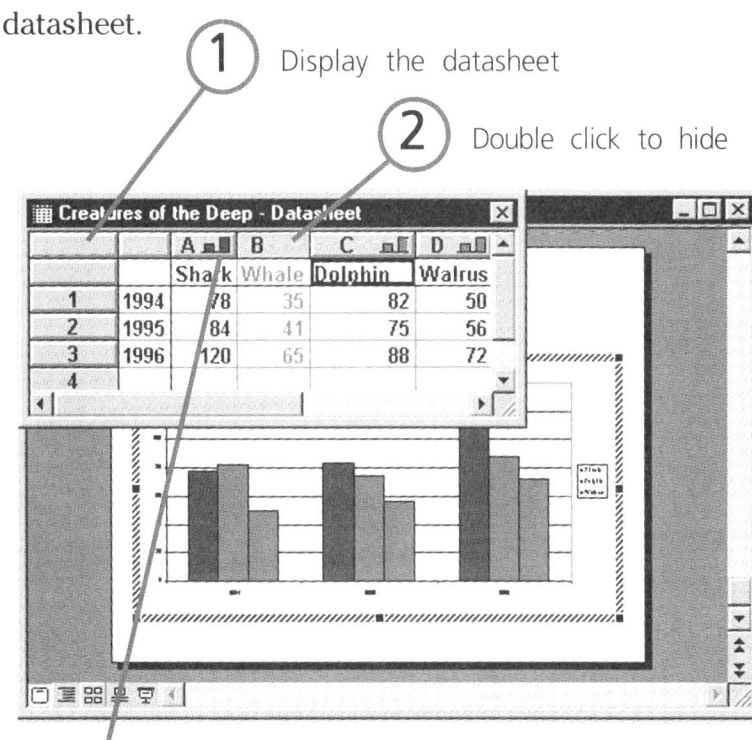

① Display the datasheet

② Double click to hide

Data series by column

Take note

You can easily control which toolbars to display. Right click on a toolbar that is currently open, and at the list of toolbar names, tick those you wish to display. If you switch all the toolbars off, open the View menu and choose Toolbars to switch them back on again!

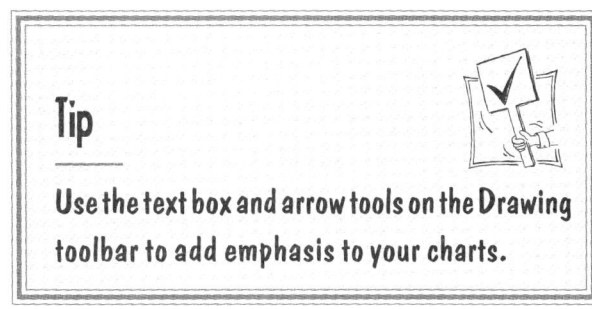

Tip

Use the text box and arrow tools on the Drawing toolbar to add emphasis to your charts.

Colours and patterns

If you don't like the colour of a data series – the bars representing one set of data on your chart – try experimenting with the options available.

① Select the data series

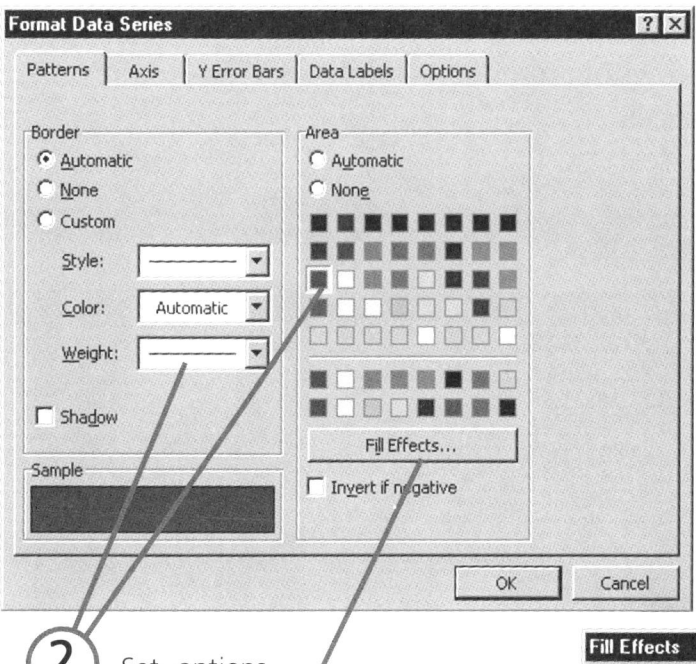

② Set options

③ Click Fill Effects...

Basic steps

1 Double click on a item (e.g. bar or line) in the data series.

2 On the **Patterns** tab of the **Format Data Series** dialog box select the options required.

3 If you want a pattern, click **Fill Effects...**

4 Experiment with the Fill Effects until you find something you like.

5 Click [OK] then [OK] again to exit.

④ Experiment!

⑤ Click OK

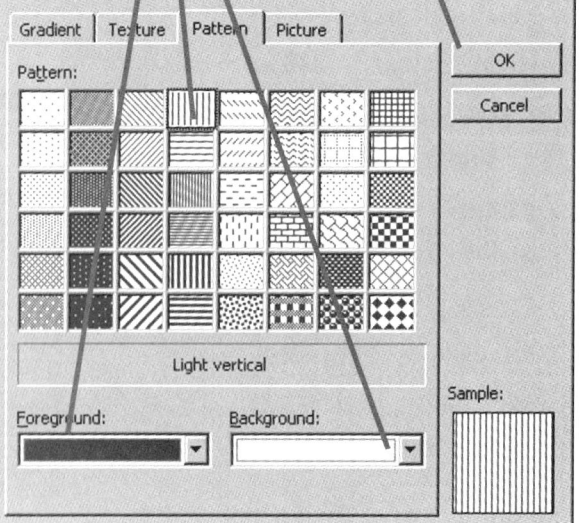

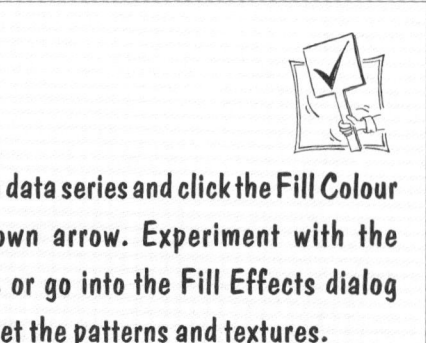

Tip

Select a data series and click the **Fill Colour** drop down arrow. Experiment with the colours, or go into the **Fill Effects** dialog box to get the patterns and textures.

Leaving Graph 97

When your chart is complete, click anywhere on the slide outside its placeholder to return to your presentation.

When you leave the Graph 97 environment, the whole chart becomes an object within your presentation, and can be moved, copied, deleted or resized as necessary.

Tip

If you wish to take your chart back into the graphic environment, simply double click on it.

Name of presentation

Legend

Arrow and text box added using drawing tools

Value axis

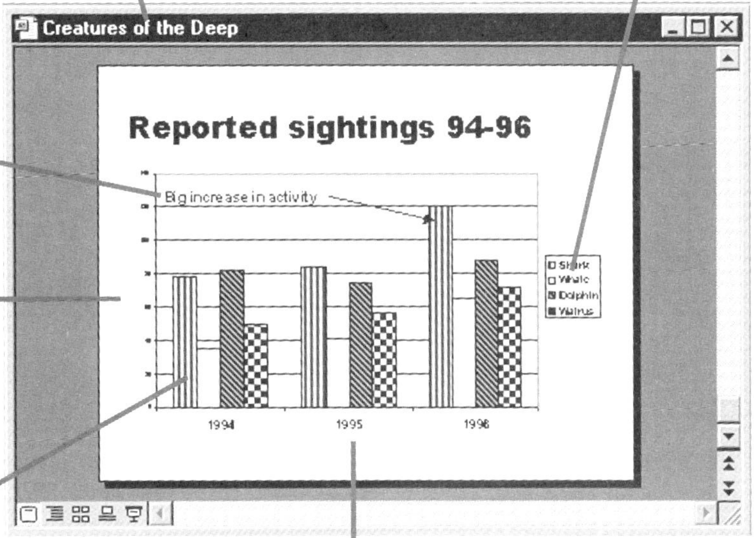

Creatures of the Deep

Reported sightings 94-96

Big increase in activity

Shark
Whale
Dolphin
Walrus

1994   1995   1996

Use strongly patterned fill styles if the chart's slide is to be printed in black and white

Category axis

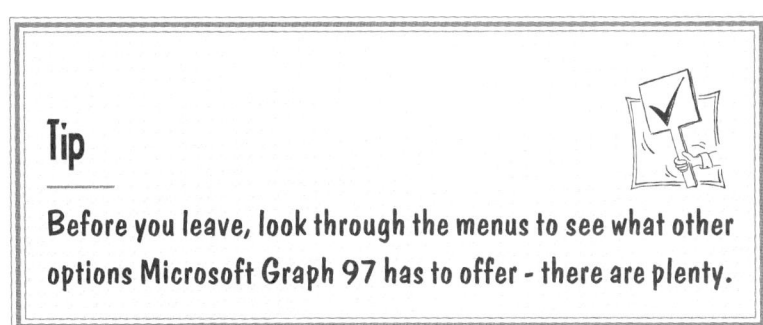

Tip

Before you leave, look through the menus to see what other options Microsoft Graph 97 has to offer - there are plenty.

Summary

- ❑ **Charts** can be used on any of your slides.

- ❑ Working in the **Microsoft Graph97** environment is similar to working and charting in Excel.

- ❑ The data you wish to chart is entered into a **datasheet**.

- ❑ The data series can be in rows or columns.

- ❑ There are several **chart types** to choose from – bar, line, area, etc.

- ❑ **Colours**, **patterns**, **text** and **drawing** can all be used to enhance your charts.

- ❑ The **formatting** of any object can be edited easily.

- ❑ When you **leave Microsoft Graph 97**, the chart that you have created is displayed on your slide.

- ❑ You can **double click** on your chart **to take it back** into the Microsoft Graph 97 environment to edit it.

8 More objects...

Organization charts

Organization charts give you another opportunity to make your point using a diagram rather than words.

This section introduces Organization Chart and some of its features. If you use a lot of organization charts, tour through its menus and the on-line Help to appreciate its full potential.

You have a choice on how to get into Organization Chart to set your details up:

● Choose a slide from the New Slide dialog box that has an Organization Chart placeholder on it;

or

● Choose a slide with an Object placeholder on it.

❏ With an Organization chart placeholder

1 Double click within the Organization chart placeholder on your slide.

① Double click in the chart placeholder

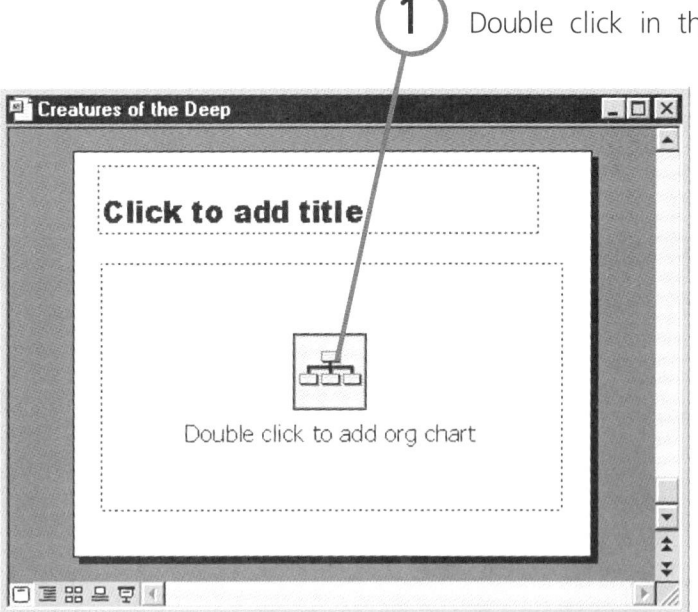

Tip

Work out the structure you wish to display before you start.

Basic steps

❏ With an object placeholder

1 Double click within the object placeholder on your slide to open the **Insert Object** dialog box.

2 Choose **MS Organization Chart 2.0**.

3 Click ⬛ OK ⬛.

Tip

Don't try to display too large a structure – the finished slide should be clear and easily understood.

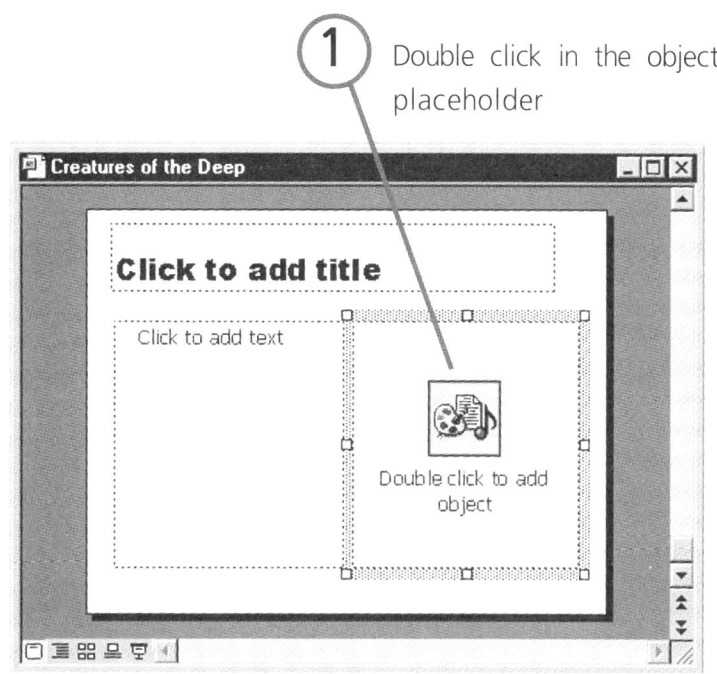

① Double click in the object placeholder

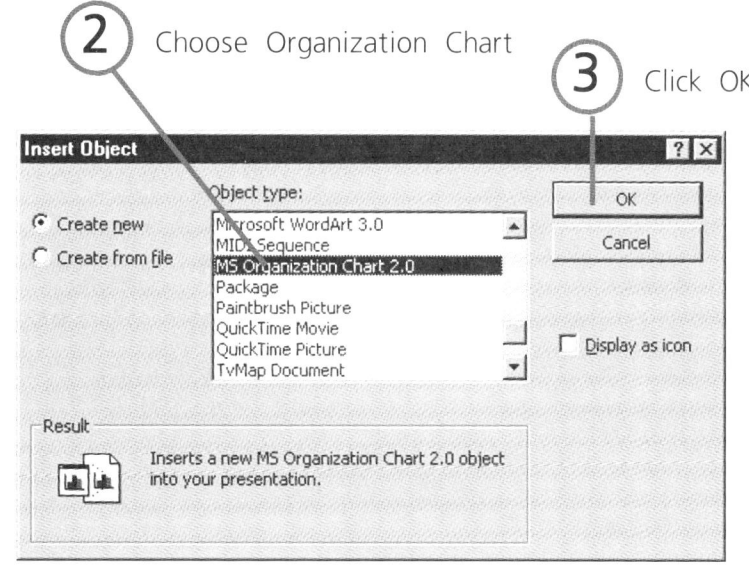

② Choose Organization Chart

③ Click OK

85

Text and boxes

The Organization Chart window

Organization charts can be very complicated structures but they have only simple elements. The small set of tools in this window are all that you need. Most are for adding boxes, and all the normal range of relationships are covered here.

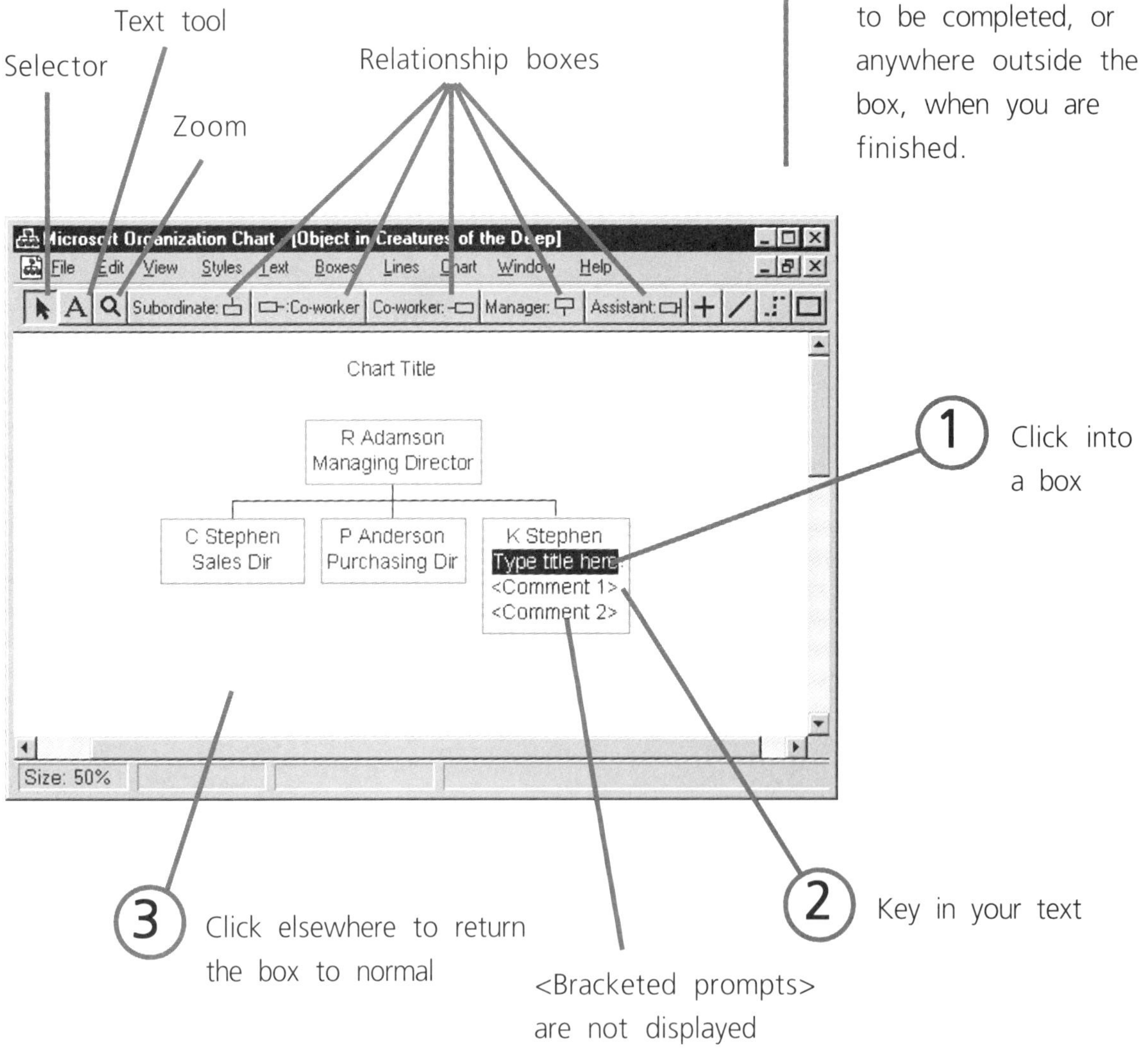

1 Click in the box you wish to write in.

2 Key in your data and press [Enter] or the arrow keys to move to the next row.

3 Click on the next box to be completed, or anywhere outside the box, when you are finished.

Selector

Text tool

Zoom

Relationship boxes

Microsoft Organization Chart - [Object in Creatures of the Deep]

File   Edit   View   Styles   Text   Boxes   Lines   Chart   Window   Help

Subordinate: □-:Co-worker   Co-worker: -□   Manager: Assistant:□   +   /   .:   □

Chart Title

R Adamson
Managing Director

C Stephen
Sales Dir

P Anderson
Purchasing Dir

K Stephen
Type title here
<Comment 1>
<Comment 2>

Size: 50%

(1) Click into a box

(2) Key in your text

(3) Click elsewhere to return the box to normal

<Bracketed prompts> are not displayed

86

Basic steps

Adding and deleting boxes

❑ **To Add a box**

1 Select the box type from the Toolbar.

2 Click on the box to which the new box is related.

You can easily build your chart up by adding boxes where needed. Deleting boxes is even easier.

● You can add several boxes simultaneously – see the Tip below.

① Select a box type

② Click on the related box

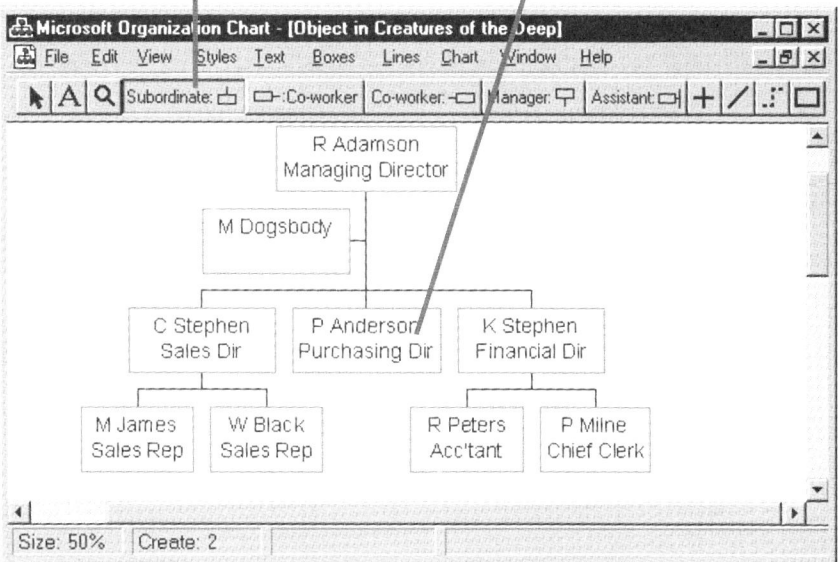

Take note

To delete a box, click on it to select it, and press **[Delete]**. If you change your mind, use Edit – Undo to bring it back.

Tip

To relate several boxes to an existing box simultaneously, click the box type required the number of times you need it – if you want to add 3 boxes click 3 times – then click the box to which the new boxes are related.

Text and drawing tools

The text and drawing tools can be used to add the finishing touches to your organisation chart. If you need text outside the boxes on your chart, use the Text tool.

❏ Text

1 Click the Text tool.

2 Click to position the insertion point.

3 Key in the text.

4 Click anywhere outside the text area to deselect the text.

1 Click the Text tool

2 Place the I-beam

3 Key in text

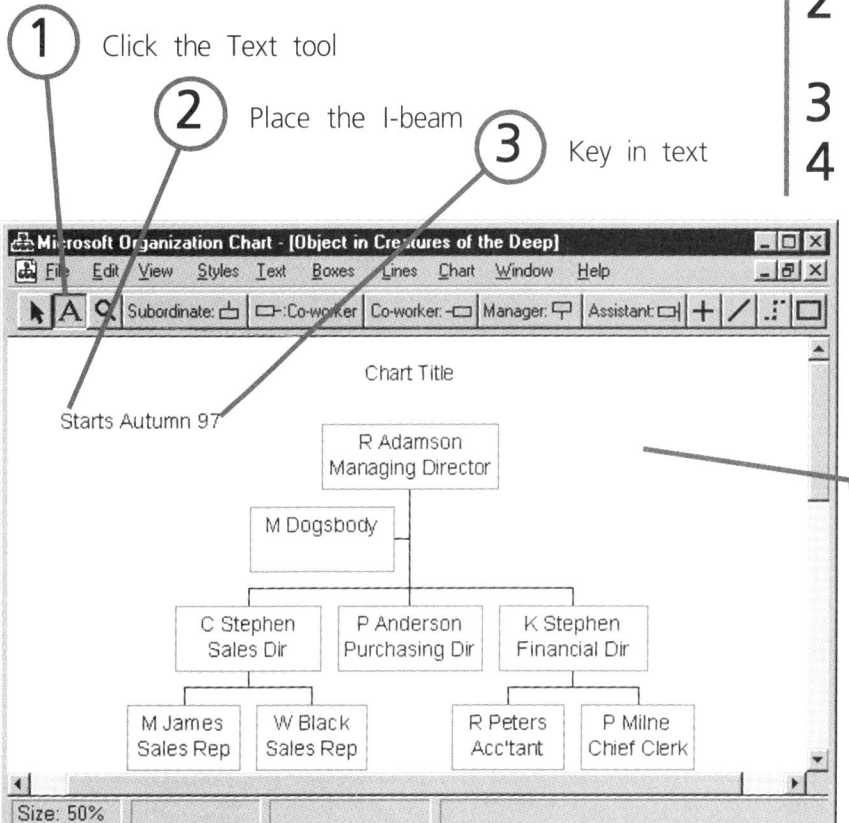

4 Click anywhere

The Drawing tools

There are four drawing tools – three types of line and a box. These are all you need to build an organization chart.

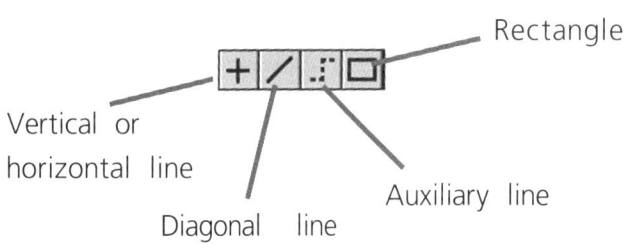

Rectangle

Vertical or horizontal line

Diagonal line

Auxiliary line

88

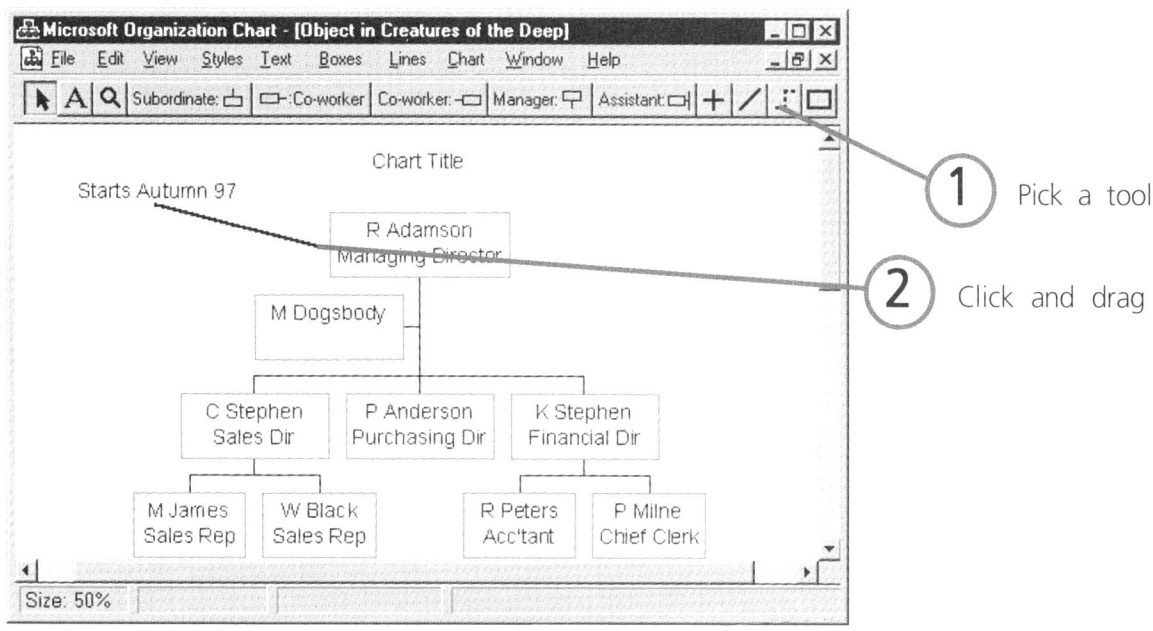

1 Pick a tool

2 Click and drag

❏ Chart title

Chart title

1 Select the Chart Title prompt.

2 Key in the title.

or

Press [Delete] to remove the prompt.

You can give your chart a title here or in the Slide Title area, back in your presentation. If you opt to key in the title in the presentation, delete the Chart Title prompt.

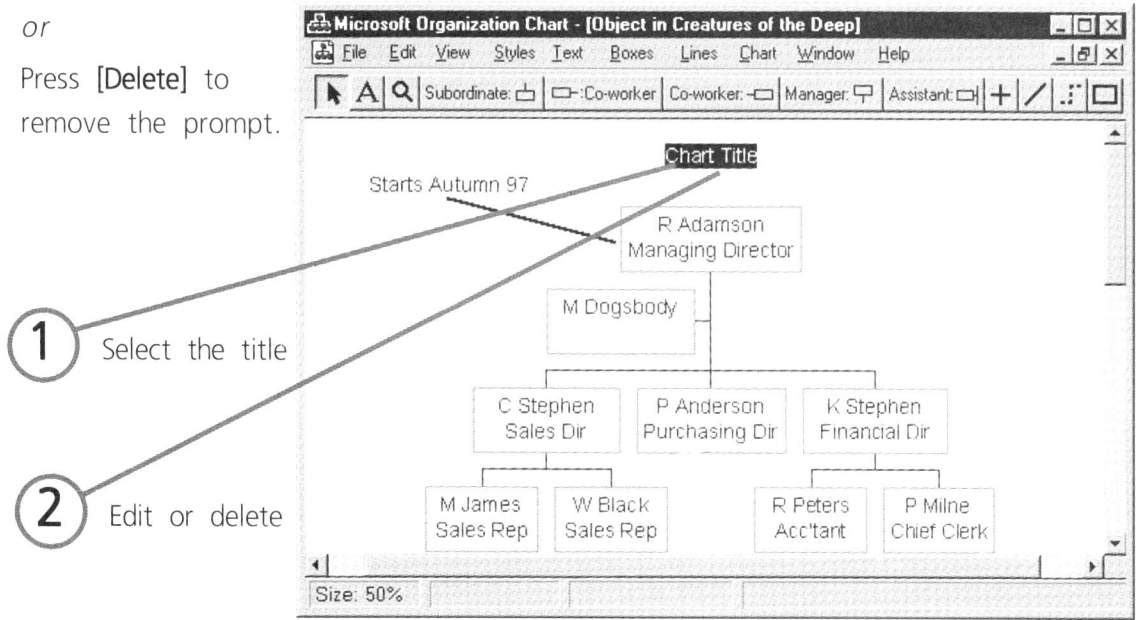

1 Select the title

2 Edit or delete

Zoom options

You can zoom in and out on your organization chart to get a closer look at what's there, or to get an overview of the whole thing. There are 4 options:

● Size to Window – for an overview of the whole chart;

● 50% of Actual – the best mode for normal work;

● Actual Size (100%) – in this mode the Zoom tool toggles to Size to Window;

● 200% of Actual – if you want to get really close.

❑ Zoom to Actual size

1 Click 🔍 the **Zoom** tool.

2 Click where you want to zoom in on.

❑ **Zoom out**

1 Select ⛁ the **Size to Window** tool.

2 Click on the chart – it reduces so you can see the entire chart.

Click to Zoom out – the button toggles back to 🔍

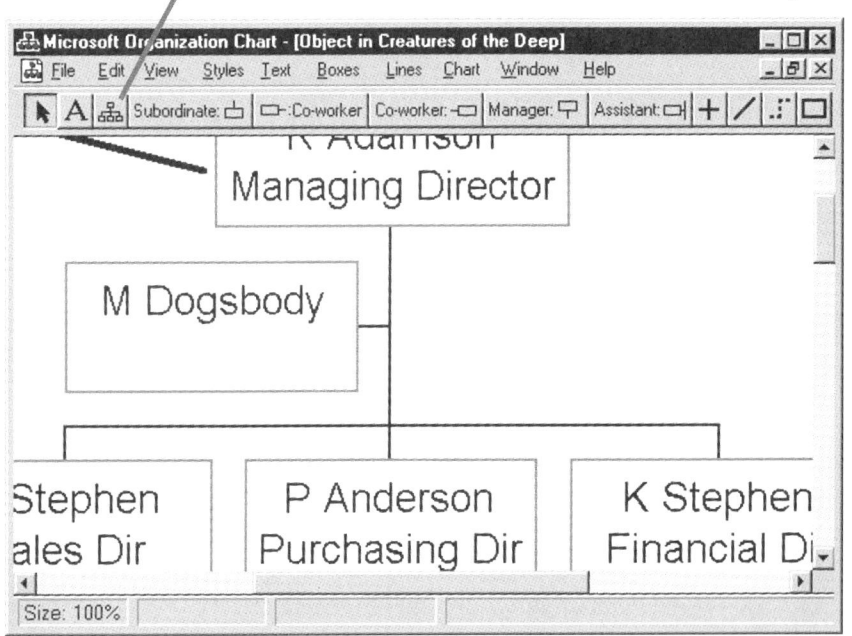

① Open the View menu

② Select 50% of Actual

❑ **Return to Normal**

1 Open the **View** menu.

2 Select **50% of Actual**.

❏ **To restyle a box**

1 Select the box(es).

2 Open the **Boxes** menu and choose **Border**, **Shadow** or **Colour**.

3 Select an option.

❏ **To edit lines**

4 Select the line(s).

5 From the **Lines** menu choose **Thickness**, **Style** or **Colour**

6 Select an option.

Using the Boxes, Lines and Text menus, you can add the finishing touches to your organisation chart – edit the line styles, add shadows to the boxes, change the colour, size and font of text, etc.

② Open the Boxes menu

① Select the box

③ Set the option

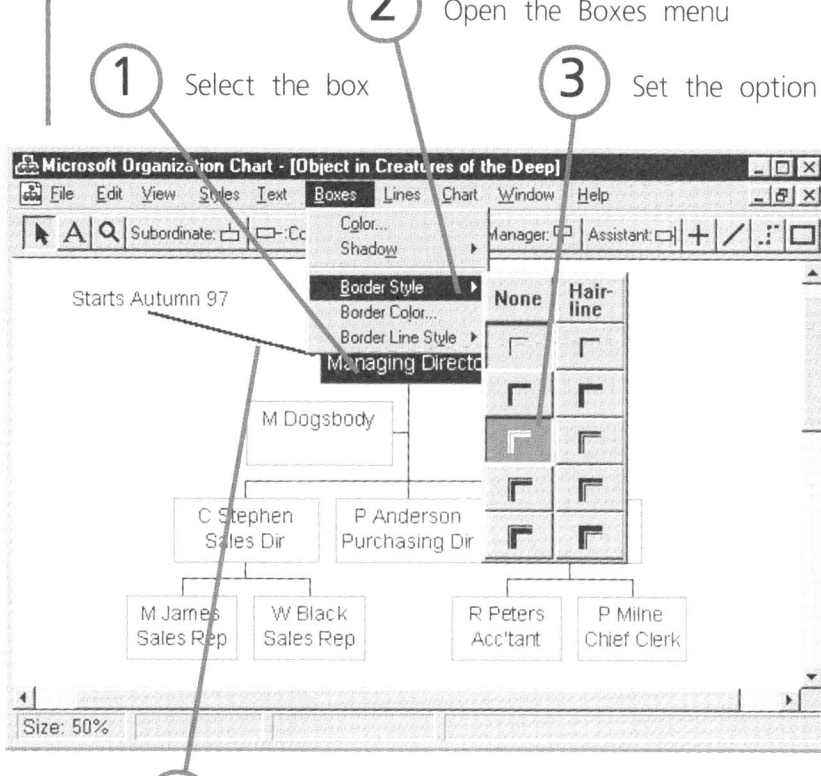

④ Select the line

Tip

To select several boxes or lines at once, select one then hold [Shift], and click on the others.

⑤ What do you want to edit?

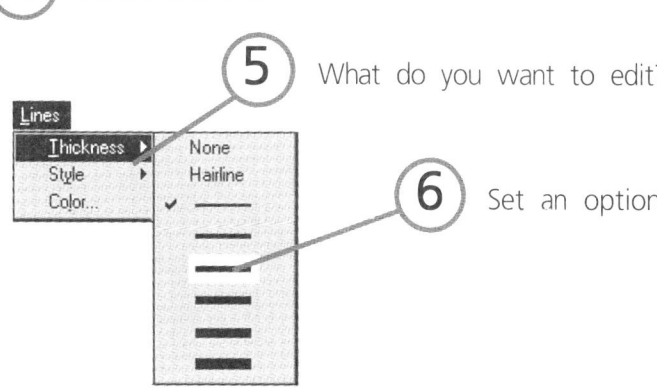

⑥ Set an option

Update and exit

Once you've completed your organisation chart, you will need to update the slide in your presentation and return to the presentation proper to continue working on it.

Exit Organization Chart as you do any Windows application.

1 Open the File menu.

2 Choose **Exit and Return** to *presentation name.*

3 Click **Yes** to update your presentation, before exiting.

or

4 Open the **File** menu.

5 Choose **Update** *presentation name.*

Your slide will now display your chart, but you are still in Organization Chart.

6 Click the Close button on the title bar.

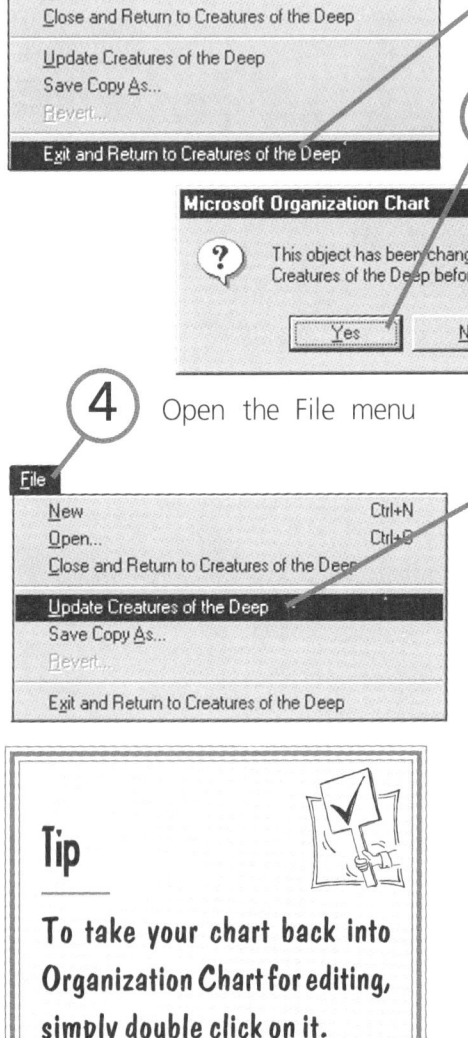

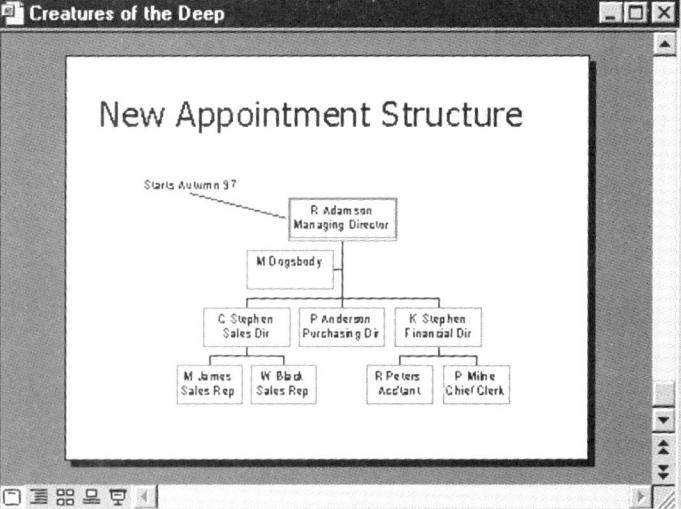

Tip

To take your chart back into Organization Chart for editing, simply double click on it.

Basic steps

❏ **Slide with placeholder**

1 Double click on the **table** placeholder on your slide.

2 Specify the number of rows and columns.

3 Click [OK].

4 Complete the table as shown on the next page.

If you are accustomed to creating tables using Word, you'll find it very easy to create tables on your slides. A table is inserted as an object.

There are several ways to get started. You could:

● Create a new slide with a table placeholder set up;

● Use the Insert Word Table tool on the standard toolbar.

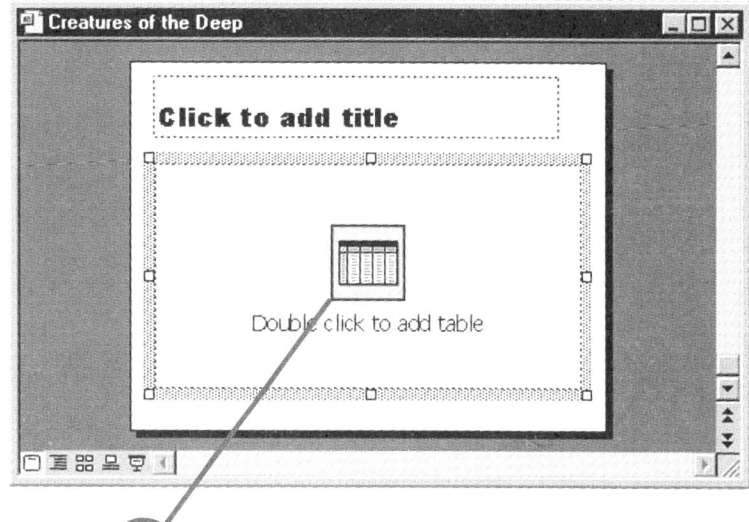

① Double click in the placeholder

② Set the table size

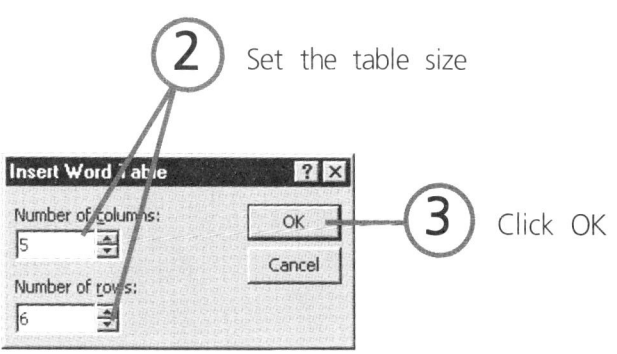

③ Click OK

Take note

When working on a table, you will notice a Table menu appear on your menu bar.

Basic steps

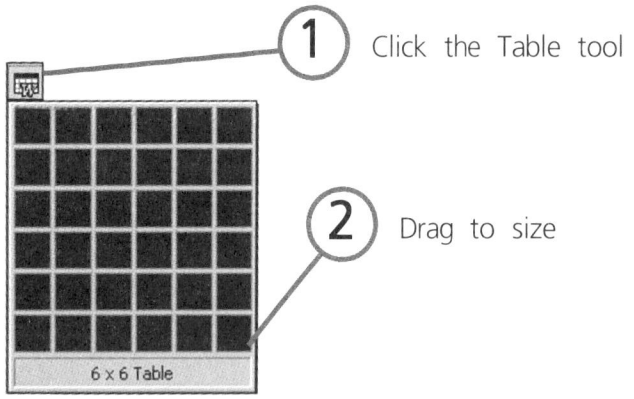

① Click the Table tool

② Drag to size

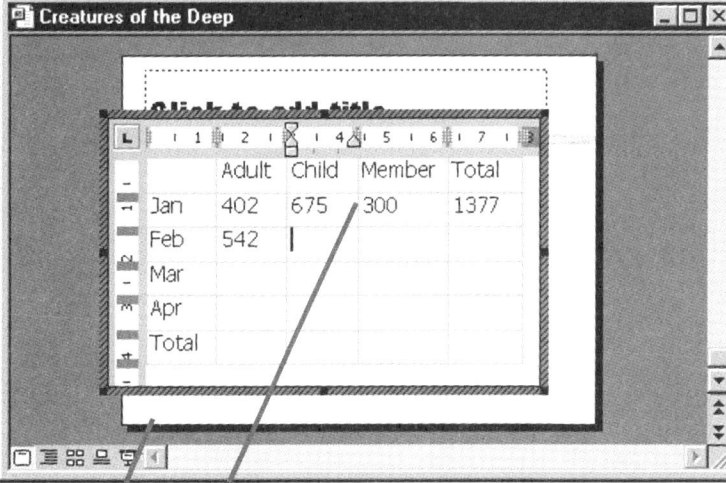

③ Key in and format data

④ Click outside when done

- ❏ Using the Insert Word Table tool

1 Click ▦ the **Insert Word Table** tool.

2 Click and drag over the grid to specify the table size required.

- ❏ Entering data

3 Complete your table using the same methods as you would in Word (note a Table menu appears).

4 Click outside the table area when done.

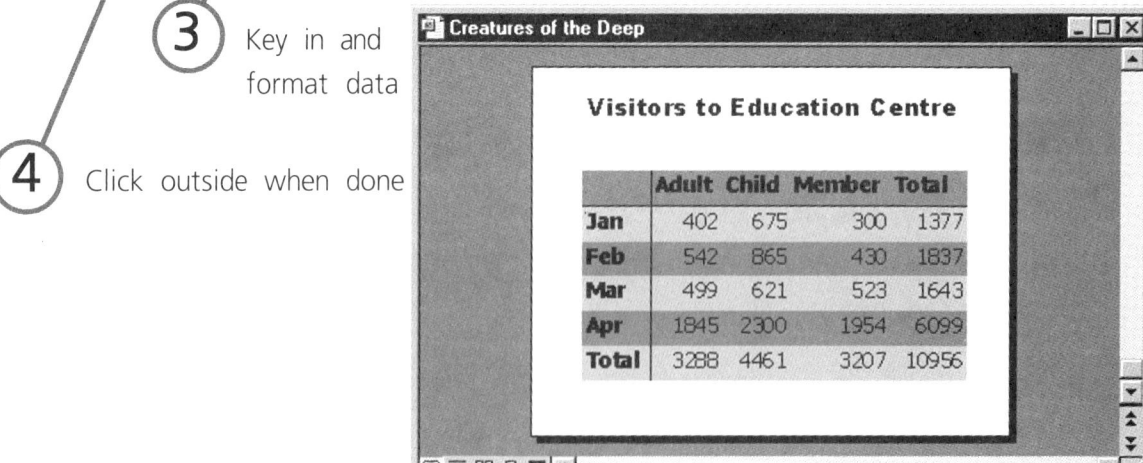

Visitors to Education Centre

	Adult	Child	Member	Total
Jan	402	675	300	1377
Feb	542	865	430	1837
Mar	499	621	523	1643
Apr	1845	2300	1954	6099
Total	3288	4461	3207	10956

Basic steps

❏ From a slide with a Clip art placeholder

1 Double click within the **Clip art** placeholder

❏ From a slide with an **Object** placeholder

2 Double click within the **object** placeholder to open the **Insert Object** dialog box

3 Choose **Microsoft Clip Gallery**

4 Click **OK**

❏ From a slide with no placeholder set

5 Click 🔲 the **Insert Clip Art** tool on the Standard toolbar

Take note

However you start, you end up Microsoft Clip Gallery 3.0, ready to choose your picture.

PowerPoint comes hundreds of Clip art pictures that can be added to your slides. If you purchased the CD version of Office 97 you will find lots of Clip art on it that isn't installed on your disk automatically.

There are three main ways of getting your hands (or mouse) on the Clip art.

● Set up a New Slide with a Clip art placeholder on it;

   or

● Choose a slide from the New Slide dialog box that has an Object placeholder already on it;

   or

● Click the Insert Clip Art tool.

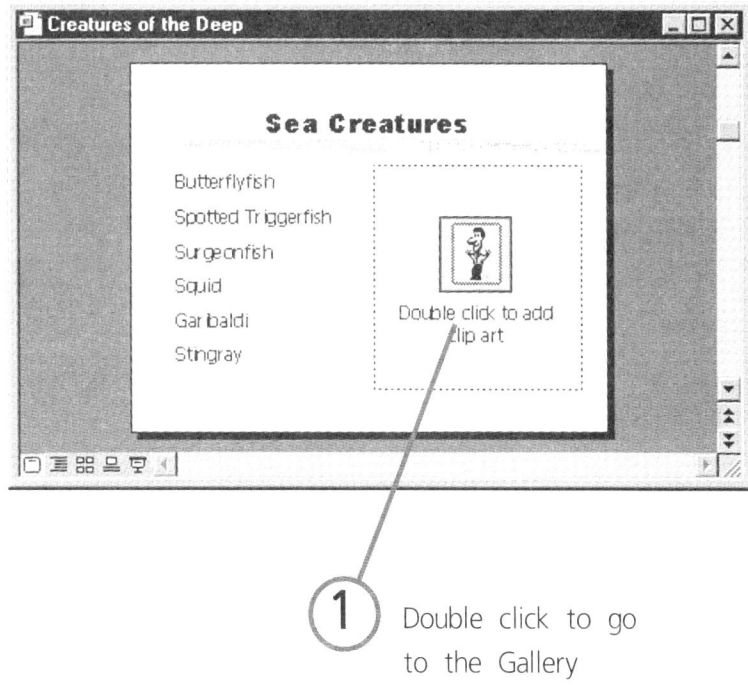

① Double click to go to the Gallery

Choosing a picture

The Clip art is organised into several categories to make it easier for you to locate pictures. Browse through them to see what is available. Once you have selected the category, thumbnail images are displayed in the preview window. Simply choose the one that best suits your purposes.

1 Scroll through the **Categories:** to find a set.

2 Click on the **Category** name to select it.

3 Scroll through the **Pictures** until you see the one you want.

4 Click on the picture to select it.

5 Click **Insert**.

The Gallery has more than just Clip Art

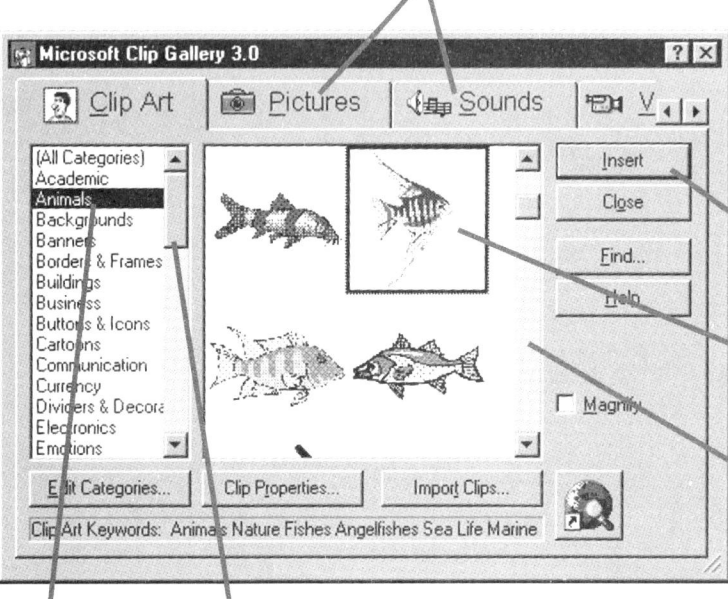

⑤ Insert it

④ Select a picture

③ See what's there

① Scroll through the Categories

② Click to select

Tip

You can double click on a picture, to add it to your slide.

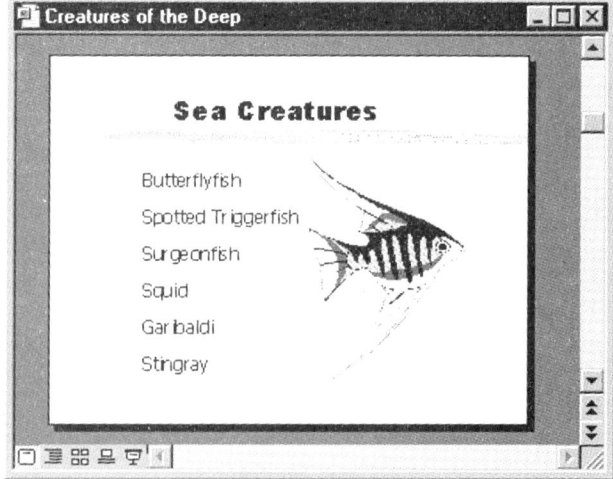

Fine tuning the picture

Tip

Use the Clip Art, Drawing and Text tools to create less formal slides!

Pictures can be edited in the same way as other objects.

After you have clicked on a picture to select it, you can...

● Press [**Delete**] to delete the object;

● Click and drag any of the handles around the edges of the picture to resize it;

● Click and drag the edge (not a handle) to move it;

● Use the Picture toolbar to create special effects.

Deselect it by clicking anywhere off it.

The Picture toolbar

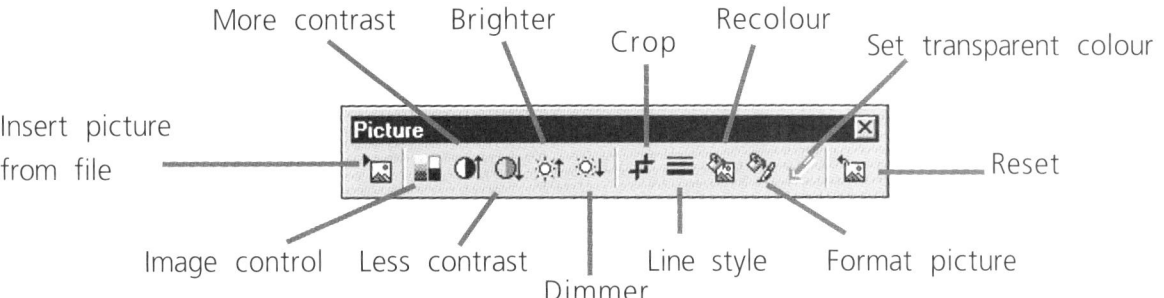

More contrast   Brighter   Crop   Recolour   Set transparent colour

Insert picture from file   Reset

Image control   Less contrast   Line style   Format picture

Dimmer

Have a look through the other tabs in the Clip Gallery

Take note

If you have Office 97 on CD, insert the CD to get the full range of Clip Art.

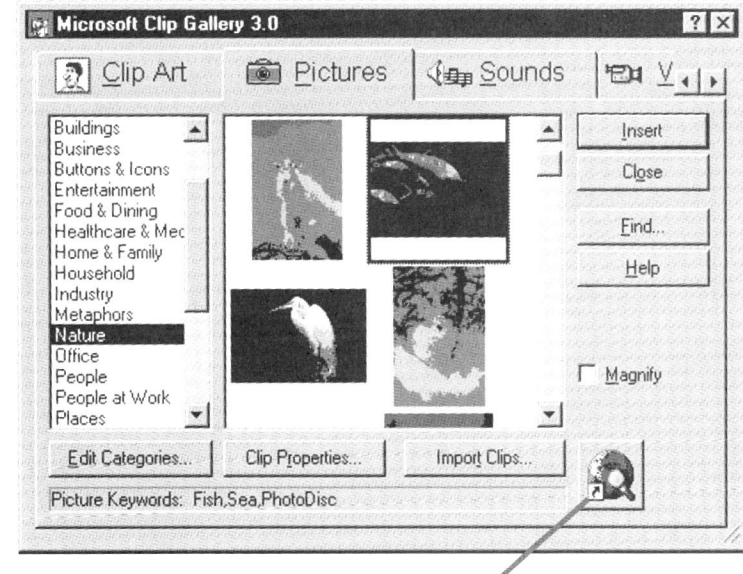

Connect via the Internet to Microsoft's on-line Gallery

Sound and video clips

If your computer has multimedia capabilities, you might want to add music or video to your presentation. There are several sounds and movies supplied with Office 97 that may be useful or you could include something from your own CDs or movie files.

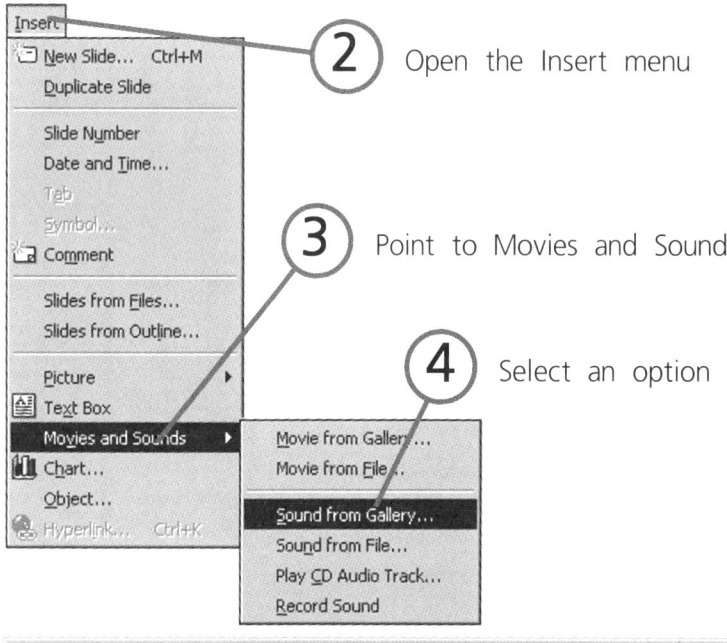

② Open the Insert menu

③ Point to Movies and Sounds

④ Select an option

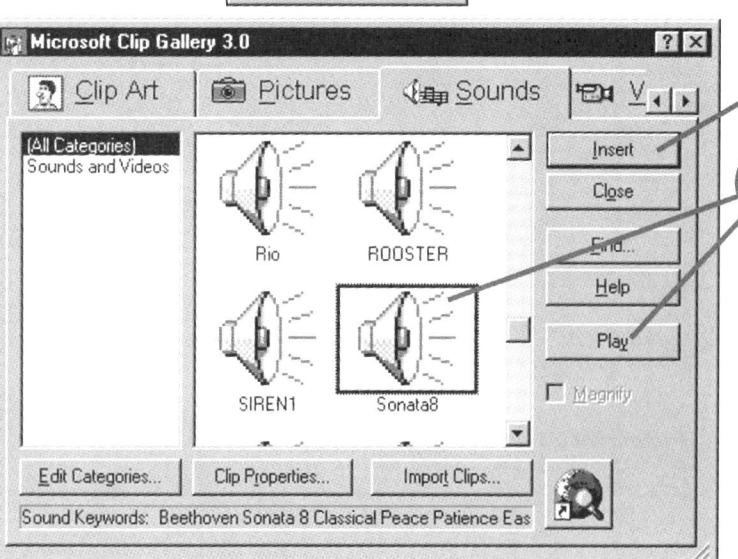

⑥ Click Insert

⑤ Pick a sound – play it?

Basic steps

1 In Slide view, display the slide you want a sound clip on.

2 Open the **Insert** menu.

3 Choose **Movies and Sounds**.

4 Select an option – e.g. *Sound from Gallery*.

5 Select a sound – click [Play] to hear it.

6 Click [Insert].

7 The sound clip icon appears in the middle of your slide – drag it into place.

8 Double click on the icon to play the sound.

Tip

To delete a sound object, select it and press [Delete].

Basic steps

Music from a CD

1 Insert your CD into the CD drive. If it starts to play, stop it and close the CD dialog box.

2 From the **Insert** menu choose **Movies and Sounds**, then **Play CD Audio Track**.

3 Set the **Start** and **End** track.

4 Click OK .

5 Drag the Play CD icon into place.

❏ To play the track(s), double click 🔊.

❏ To stop playing, click on the icon once.

You can also select a clip from one of your own CDs.

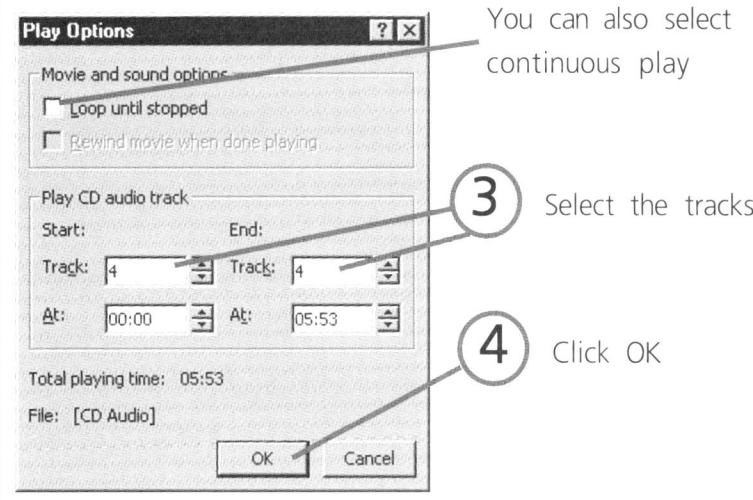

You can also select continuous play

③ Select the tracks

④ Click OK

Video clips

You can add Video clips to your presentation in the same way – choose **Movie from Gallery** or **Movie from File** from the Movies and Sounds submenu.

Take note

To edit the settings for an audio or video object, right click on the object and choose **Edit Sound Object** or **Edit Movie Object** from the shortcut menu. Complete the dialog box as required.

Globe.avi video from the Microsoft Clip Gallery

Summary

❑ **Organization Charts** can easily be added to slides.

❑ **Boxes** are added to and deleted from organisation charts as required.

❑ **Text** and **drawing tools** are available to further enhance your chart.

❑ There are several **Zoom** options so you can get a close up look or an overview of your chart.

❑ The **colour** and **format** of items on your chart can be controlled from the Boxes and Text menus.

❑ Remember to **Update your presentation** before exiting Organization Chart.

❑ Word **tables** can be created on your slides very easily.

❑ **Word menus** and **toolbars** are used when working on your table in PowerPoint.

❑ The **Clip gallery** contains pictures, photographs, sounds and movies.

❑ You can **move**, **resize** or **delete** the Clip art object once it is on your slide.

❑ You can easily add **CD** or other **sound clips**, or **video clips** into your presentation.

9 Masters

Slide Master

The Slide Master holds the formatted placeholders for the slide title and text. Changes to the Slide Master will be reflected in every slide in your presentation (except the Title Slide). Any slides where you have made changes to the text formatting at slide level will be treated as exceptions and will retain the custom formatting you applied to them.

Any background objects you want to appear on every slide (like your company name or logo) should be added to the Slide Master.

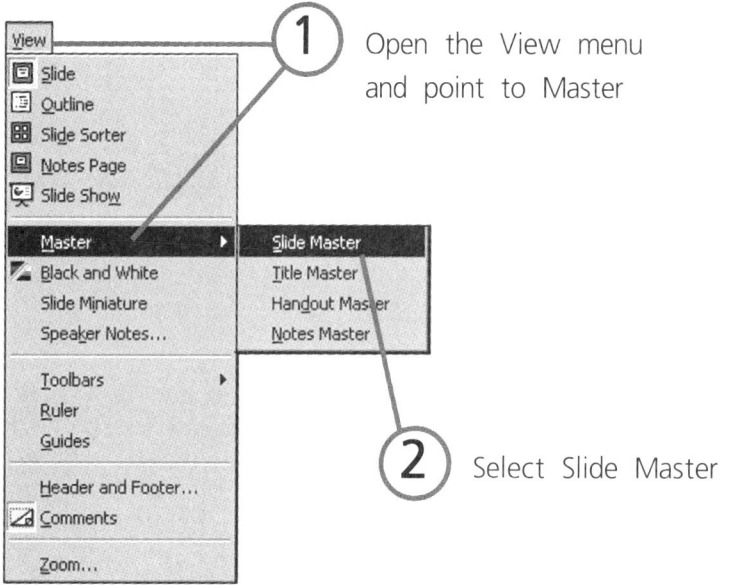

Open the View menu and point to Master

Select Slide Master

Basic steps

1 Choose **Master** from the **View** menu.

2 Select **Slide Master**.

3 Amend the Slide Master as required (using the same techniques you use on a slide in your presentation).

4 Choose an alternative view to leave your Slide Master.

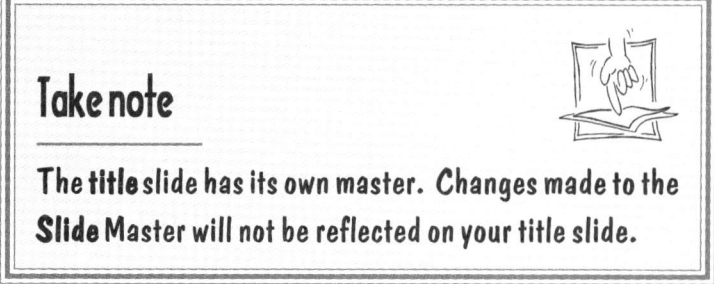

Take note

The title slide has its own master. Changes made to the Slide Master will not be reflected on your title slide.

Tip

If you hold down [Shift] and click ▢ the Slide View icon, this takes you to the Slide Master, or to the Title Master (page 104) if you are on the title slide at the time.

③ Amend the Slide Master

Font changed

Clip art added

Bullet style changed

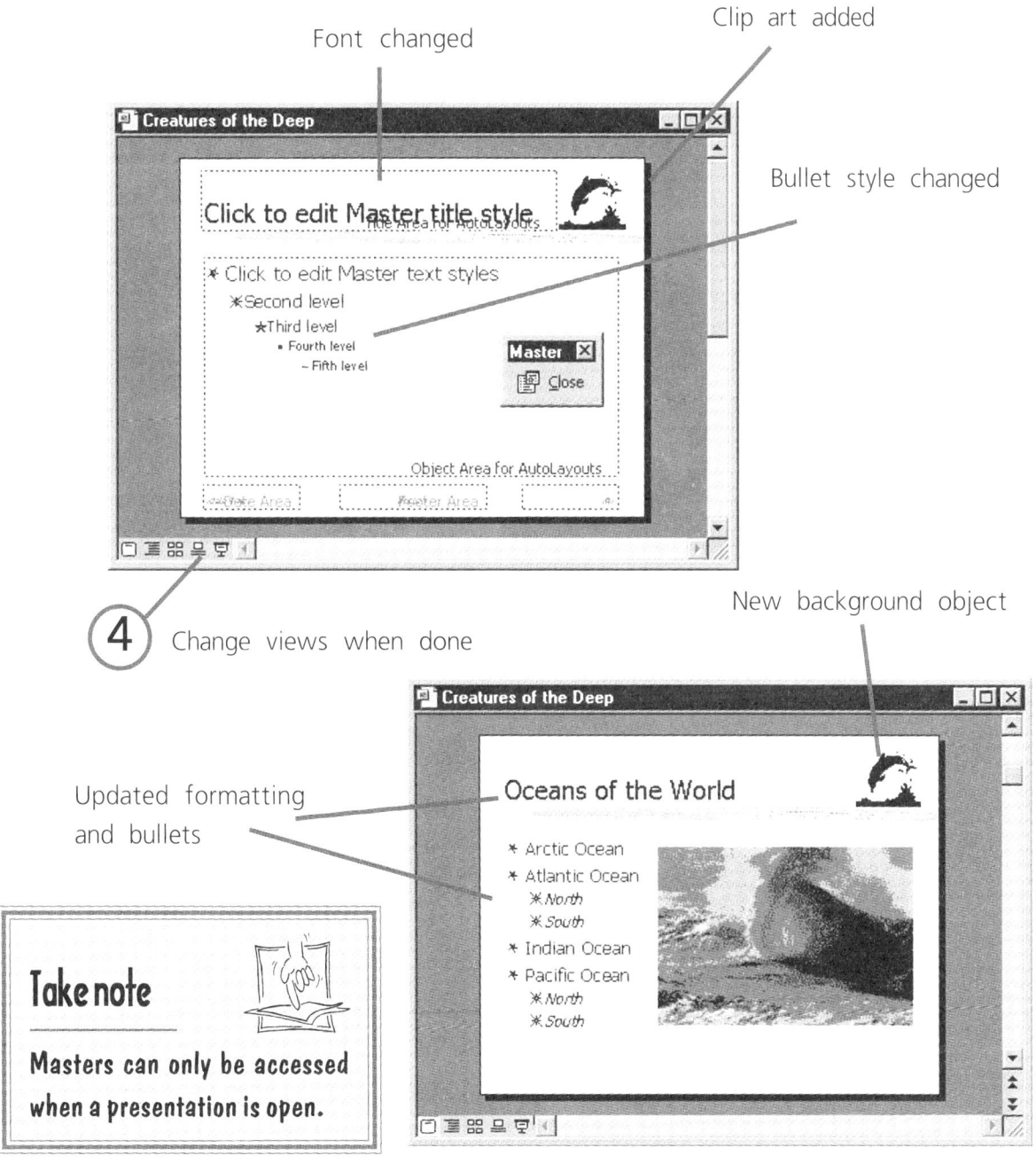

New background object

④ Change views when done

Updated formatting and bullets

Take note

Masters can only be accessed when a presentation is open.

Title Master

You can view and edit the Title Master if you wish. Changes made to the Title Master will only affect the title slide, not the others in the presentation.

1 Choose **Master** from the **View** menu.

2 Select **Title Master**.

3 Amend the Title Master as required (using the normal techniques).

4 Choose an alternative view to leave your Title Master.

(3) Edit Title Master

Font changed   ClipArt added

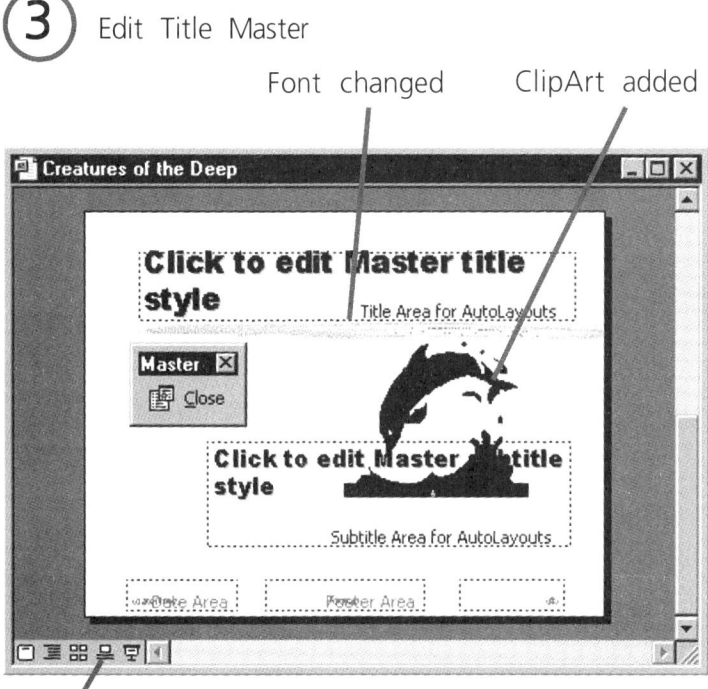

(4) Change views to end

Take note

If you are looking at the title slide in Slide view, press [Shift] and click to go into Title Master view.

Tip

You can drag the elevator to move from the Slide Master to the Title Master view.

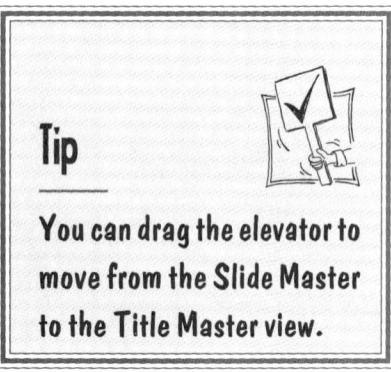

Basic steps

1 Choose **Master** from the **View** menu.

2 Select **Handout Master**.

3 Select 2, 3 or 6 slides to the page.

4 Add Clip Art if wanted.

5 Choose **Header and Footer** from the **View** menu.

6 Edit the Header and/or Footer text if necessary and click [Apply to All].

7 Choose an alternative view to leave your Handout master.

You can support your presentation with audience handouts if you wish. Handouts consist of smaller, printed versions of your slides, either two, three or six to the page (see Chapter 11 for details on printing).

If you want additional information on the handout pages – your company name or logo, the presentation title, page numbers, date, or lines for your audience to write on – add the detail to the Handout Master.

(3) Select a layout

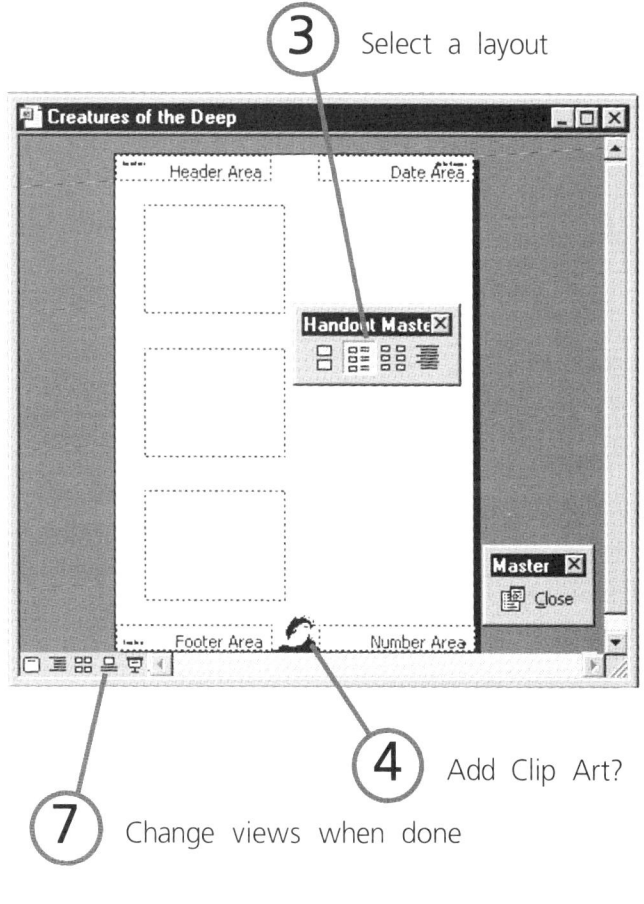

(4) Add Clip Art?

(7) Change views when done

(6) Edit as needed and Apply

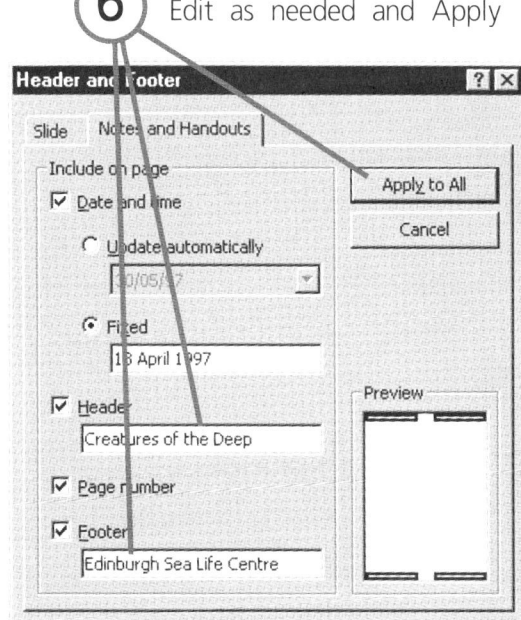

The placeholders

The Date, Page Number, Header or Footer placeholders are all optional. They can easily be deleted – or put back again if you decide you want them after all. Print a copy of your handouts and see how they look on paper before making a final decision.

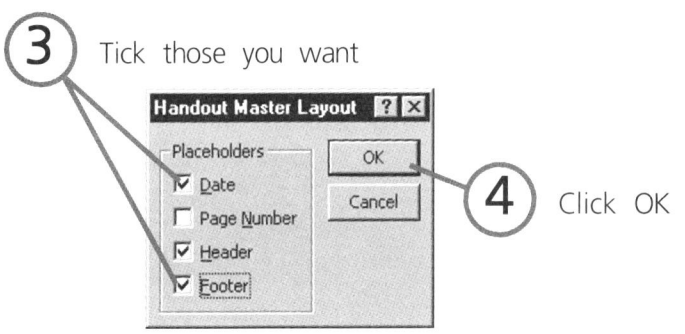

③ Tick those you want

④ Click OK

❑ Deleting placeholders

1 Select the placeholder and press [Delete].

❑ Restoring placeholders

2 Click  to open the Handout Master Layout dialog box.

3 Tick those placeholders that you want on the handouts.

4 Click **OK**.

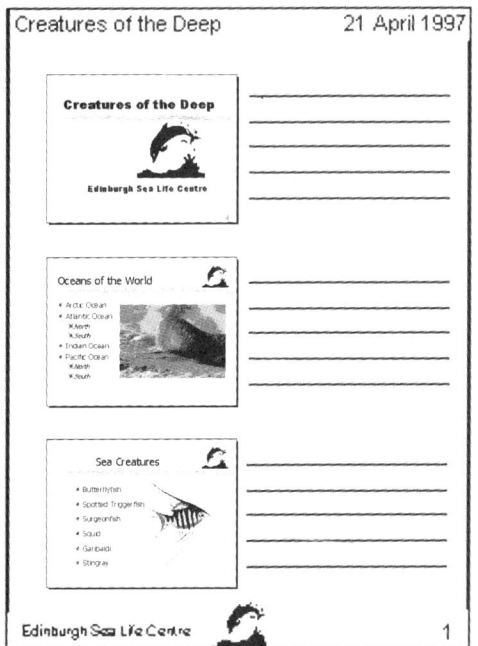

Take note

The three-slides-to-a-page layout is particularly useful if you want to leave space for your audience to make their own notes beside each slide.

Tip

To view the Handout Master, hold down [**Shift**] and click either 🔳 the Outline view or 🔡 the Slide Sorter view icon.

Basic steps

1 Choose **Master** from the **View** menu.

2 Select **Notes Master**.

3 Amend the Notes Master as required.

4 Choose an alternative view to leave your Notes Master.

Notes master

Each slide in your presentation has an accompanying notes page which consists of a smaller version of the slide along with room for any notes you want to make.

If you want to add information to your notes pages (company name or page number perhaps), or change the size of the placeholders (to allow more space for notes and less for the slide image) do so on the Notes Master.

③ Edit Notes Master

Placeholders resized

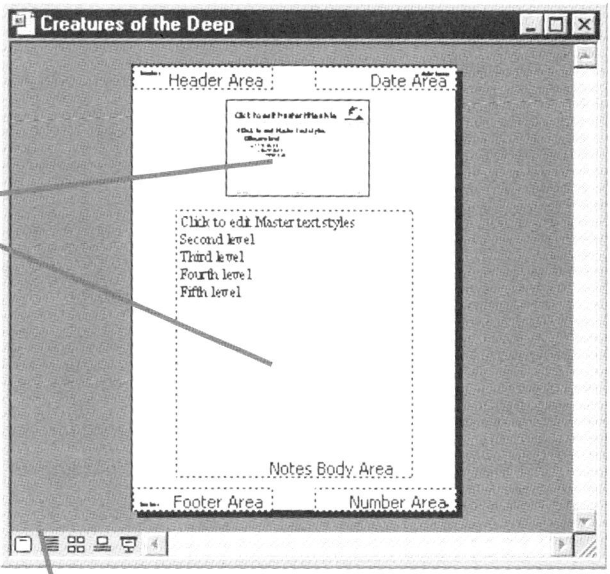

Creatures of the Deep

Header Area | Date Area

Click to edit Master title style

Click to edit Master text styles
Second level
Third level
Fourth level
Fifth level

Notes Body Area

Footer Area | Number Area

④ Change views to leave

Tip

You can view the Notes Master if you hold the [Shift] key down when you click 🖳 the Notes Pages View icon.

Summary

❏ If you want to add or **amend** an element to **every slide** (except the title slide) in your presentation, change the Slide Master, not the individual slides.

❏ If you want to add or amend an element to the **Title slide**, change the Title Master, not the individual slide.

❏ Text, graphics, page numbers, time and date fields added to the Slide, Handout and Notes Masters appear on **every slide or page**.

❏ Hold the [**Shift**] key down when you click the **View icons** to get the Masters.

10 Slide shows

Slide Sorter view

Slide Sorter view was introduced in Chapter 5 where we considered how you could rearrange the order of your slides. There are several other useful features worth exploring in Slide Sorter view, including:

- Hiding slides;
- Setting up transitions;
- Animating text on slides;
- Rehearsing timings;

We'll look at these features in this section, and see how they can help enhance your presentations.

You should be in Slide Sorter view for this section.

Slide Sorter toolbar

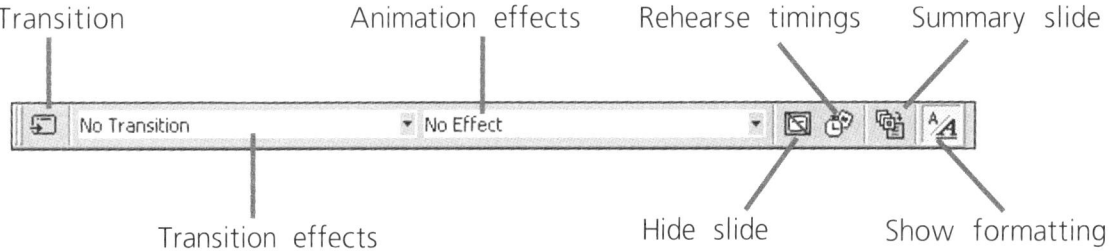

Basic steps

1 Select the slide you want to hide.

2 Click the **Hide Slide** tool.

❑ The number is crossed out under the slide.

This option can prove useful if you're not sure whether or not you will really need a particular slide for your presentation. You can include the slide in your presentation (in case it's needed), but hide it. The hidden slide will be by-passed during your slide show, unless you decide you need to use it.

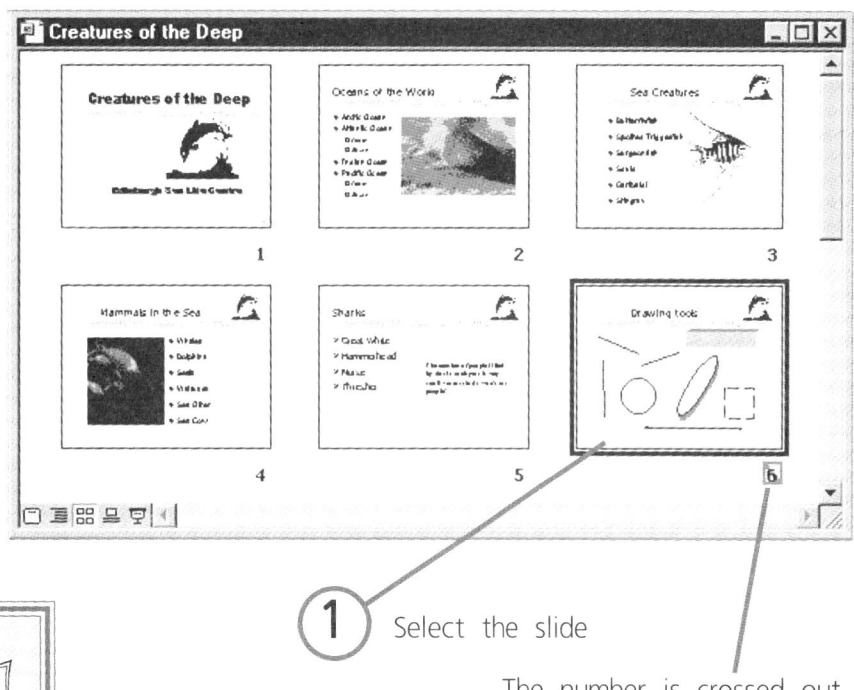

1 Select the slide

The number is crossed out

Tip

If you want to show the hidden slide during a presentation, use the Go To command, or press [H] at the slide preceding the hidden one.

Take note

To remove the hidden status from a slide, select it and click the Hide Slide tool again.

Transitions

A transition is an effect used between slides in a show. The default option is that No Transition is set, but there are some interesting alternatives you might find effective for your presentation. Experiment with the Transition options to find those best suited to your presentation.

Basic steps

1 Select the slide to which you want to specify a transition.

2 Click 🔲 the Slide Transition tool.

3 Select the **Effect** from the drop down list.

4 The Preview window demonstrates the effect – click on it to see the effect again.

5 Set the **Speed** to Fast. Focus your audiences on your slides, not the transition method!

6 Choose an **Advance** option.

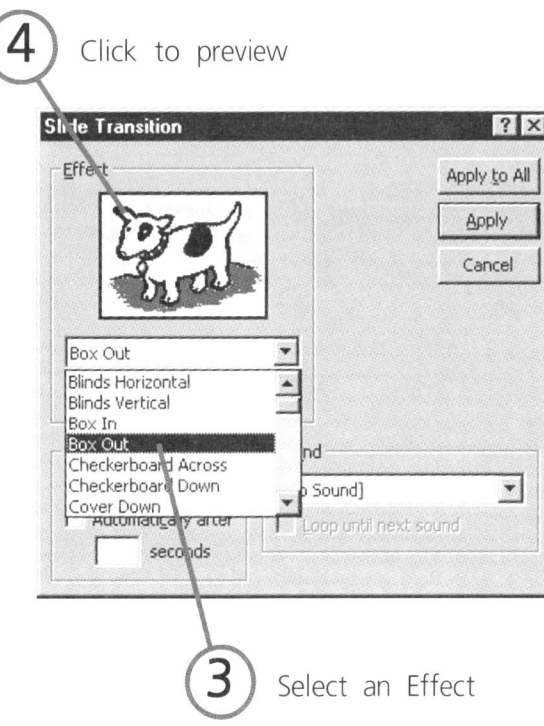

④ Click to preview

③ Select an Effect

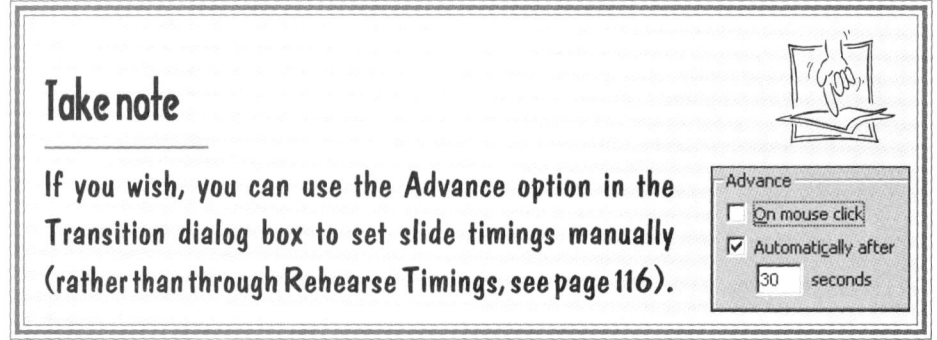

Take note

If you wish, you can use the Advance option in the Transition dialog box to set slide timings manually (rather than through Rehearse Timings, see page 116).

7 Add a **Sound** if wanted.

8 Click **Apply** or **Apply to All** if you want the effect added to all your slides.

⑤ Set the Speed

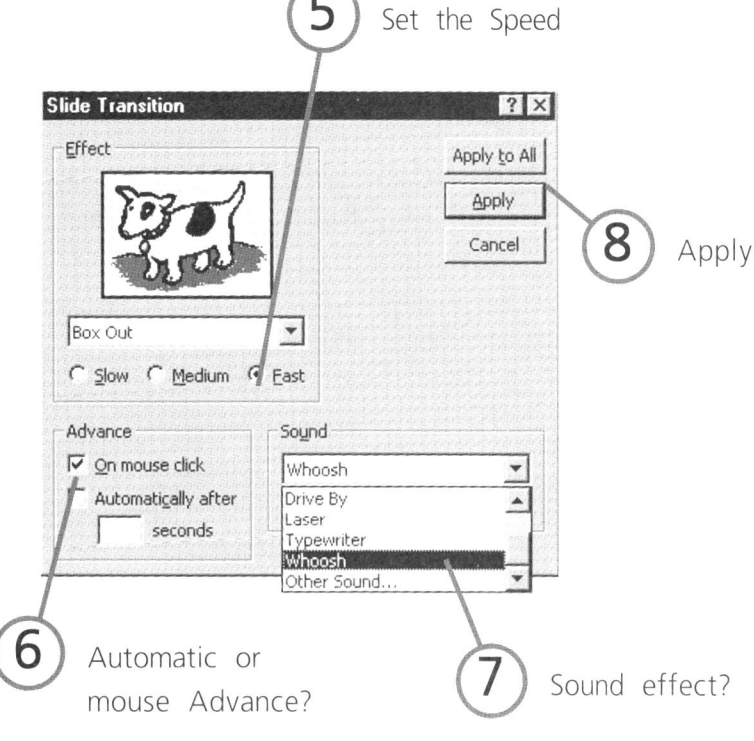

⑧ Apply

⑥ Automatic or mouse Advance?

⑦ Sound effect?

Take note

If a transition is set, a transition icon appears below the slide in Slide Sorter view. Click on it to see the transition effect.

Tip

Use the Slide Show together with Slide Sorter view when experimenting with animation effects. Then you can check that the options you choose are having the desired effect.

Preset animations

If you have several points listed on your slide, you could try building the slide up during the presentation, rather than presenting the whole list at once. Experiment with the Preset Animation options and effects until you find the ones you prefer. You can have a lot of fun messing about with the options available – but try to avoid having a different effect on each slide!

Basic steps

1 Select the slide.

2 Drop down the **Preset Animation** list on the Slide Sorter toolbar.

3 Choose an effect.

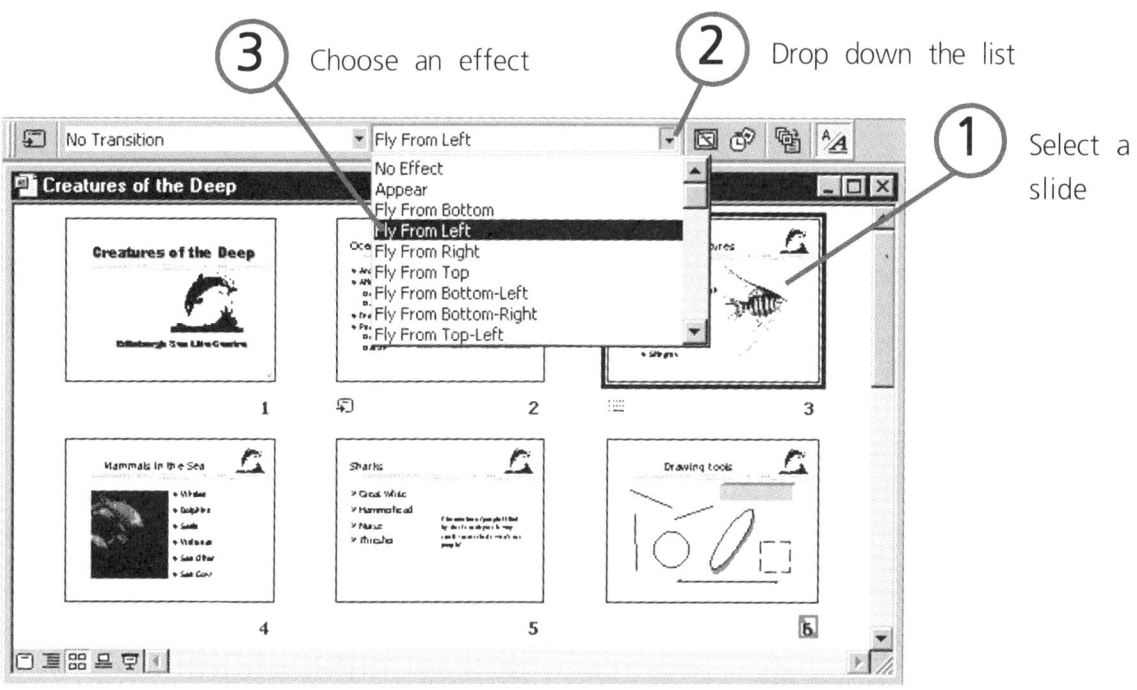

③ Choose an effect

② Drop down the list

① Select a slide

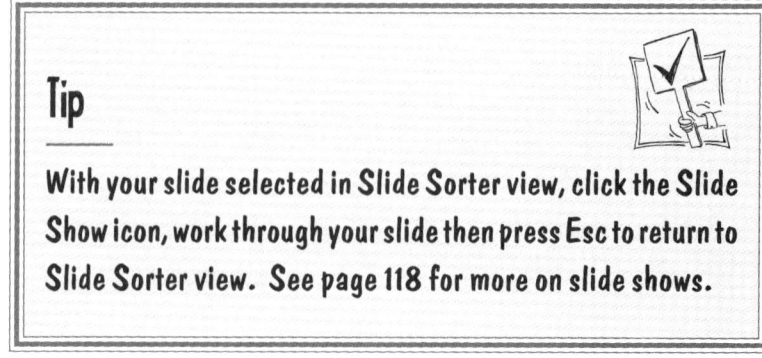

Tip

With your slide selected in Slide Sorter view, click the Slide Show icon, work through your slide then press Esc to return to Slide Sorter view. See page 118 for more on slide shows.

Basic steps

1 Select the slide (or slides) you wish to animate.

2 Choose **Preset Animation** from the **Slide Show** menu.

3 Select the option required.

Take note

You can set up your own animations (rather than use the preset ones) if you wish. You must be in Slide (not Slide Sorter) view to do this.

See Animate text and objects in the on-line help for more information.

Animation from the Slide Show menu

You can also set up your animation options through the Slide Show menu – you may find it simpler to work through these more organised menus.

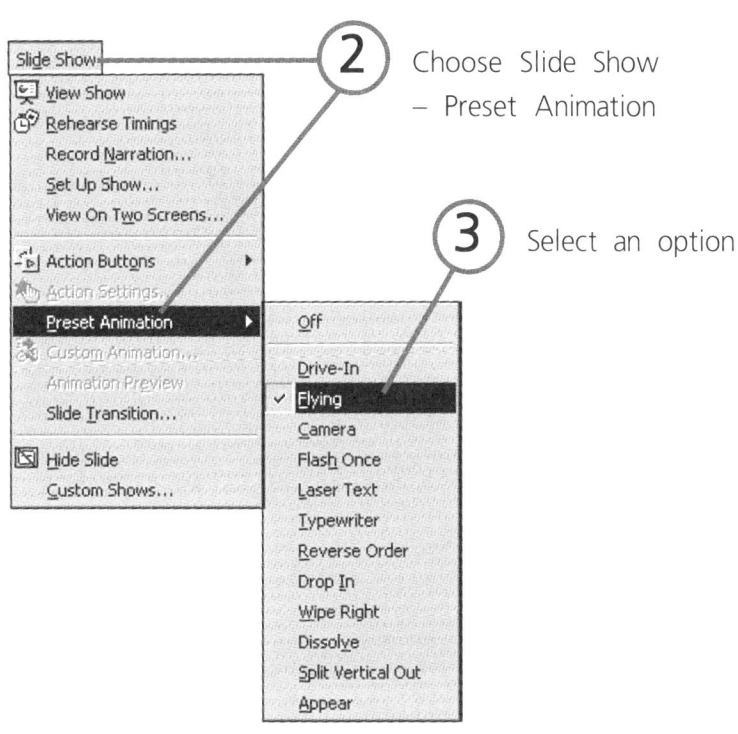

 Choose Slide Show – Preset Animation

 Select an option

Tip

You can preview your animation effects in Slide view. Display the slide that has animations set, then choose Animation Preview from the Slide Show menu. Your animation effects will be displayed in a slide miniature.

Rehearse Timings

It is a very good idea to practise your presentation before you end up in front of your audience. As well as practising what you intend to say (probably with the aid of notes you have made using the Notes Page feature), you can rehearse the timings for each slide.

Total presentation time — Current slide timing

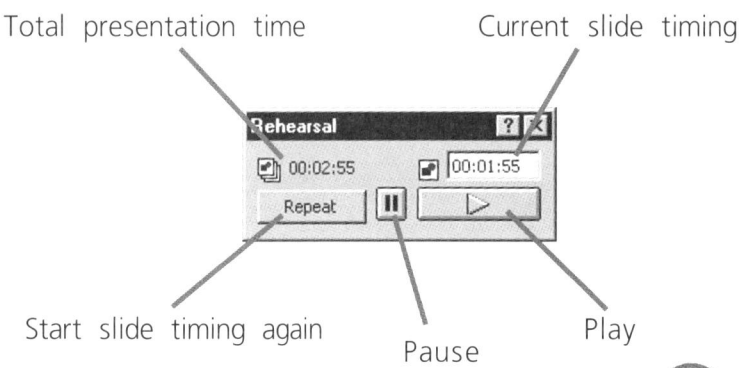

Start slide timing again — Pause — Play

1 Click the **Rehearse Timings** tool to go into your slide show for a practice run!

2 Go over what you intend to say while the slide is displayed.

3 Click the left mouse button to move to the next slide when ready.

4 Repeat steps 2 and 3 until you reach the end of your presentation.

(1) Click Rehearse Timings

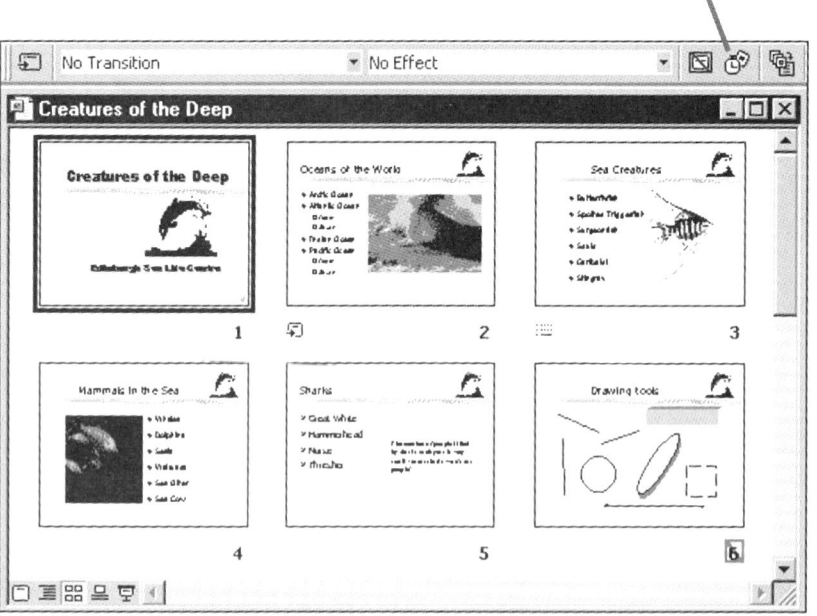

Displaying timings

A dialog box displays the total length of time your presentation took and asks if you want to record and use the new slide timings in a slide show. Choose yes, if you want each slide to advance after the allocated time.

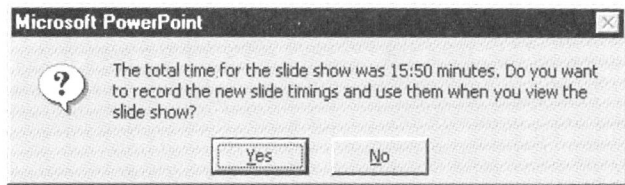

You can also have the slide timings displayed in Slide Sorter view. If you want your timings displayed choose Yes at the prompt.

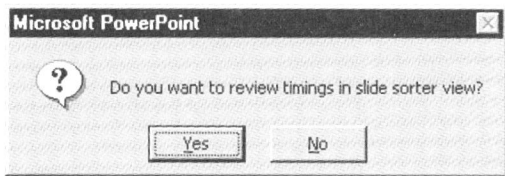

Slide timings

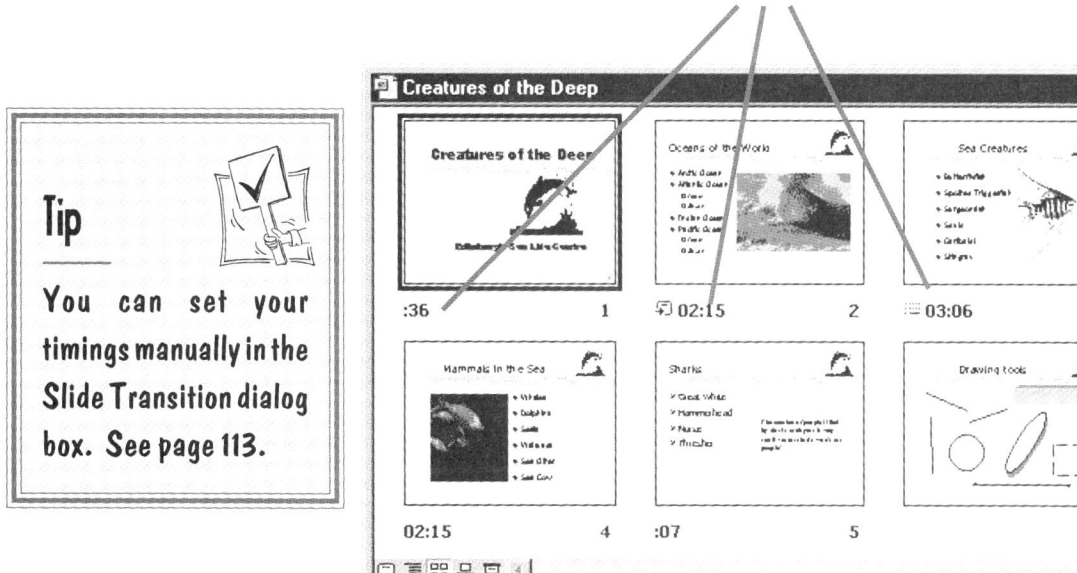

Slide Show

You can run your slide show at any time to check how your presentation is progressing. Each slide fills the whole of your computer screen.

After the last, you are returned to the view you were in when you clicked the Slide Show tool.

1 Select the slide to start from, usually the first.

2 Click  the **Slide Show** tool to the left of the status bar.

3 Press **[PageDown]** (or click the left mouse button) to move onto the next slide.

Press **[PageUp]** to move back to the previous slide if necessary.

 Select the starting slide

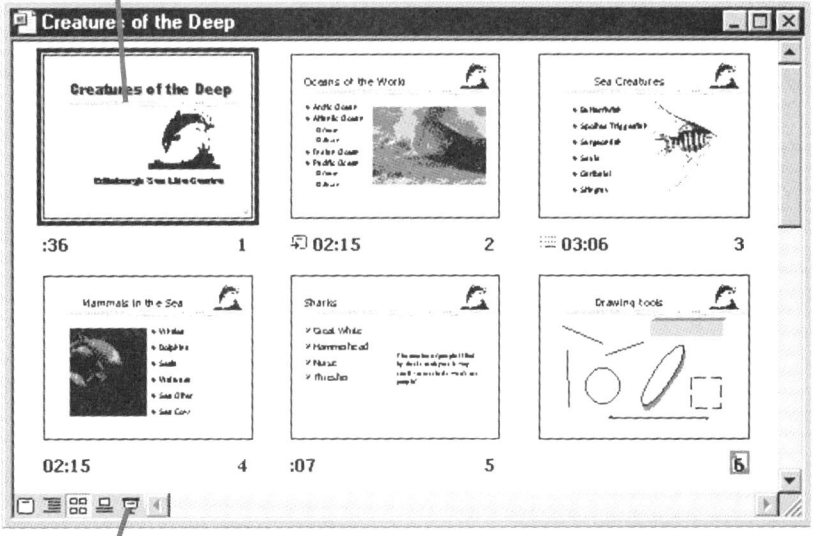

 Click Slide Show

Tip

Use the Slide Show in Slide Sorter view when experimenting with Transition and Animation effects. Then you can check that the options you choose are having the desired effect.

Take note

You can exit your slide show at any time by pressing the [Esc] key on your keyboard.

Working within your slide show

1 Click the right mouse button or  the pop-up menu icon at the bottom left corner of the screen.

❑ **To go directly to a slide**

2 Select **Go**, then **By Title**.

3 Choose the slide you want to go to.

When presenting your slide show, you might want to leave the normal sequence, go directly to a slide, or draw on the slide to focus attention. These, and other features can be accessed using the pop-up menu or the keyboard.

③ Select a slide

② Choose Go – By Title

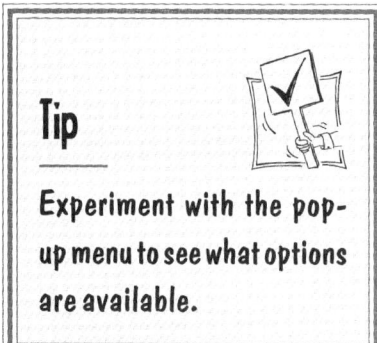

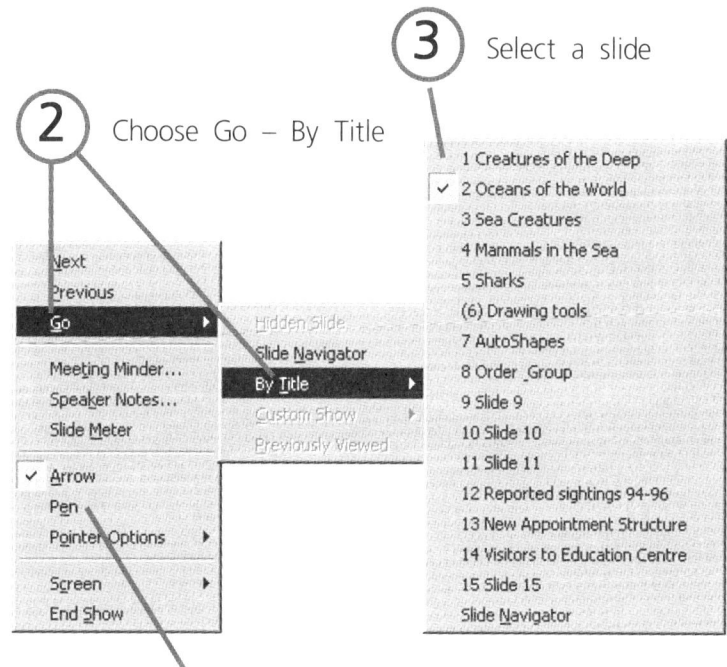

Use **Arrow** to point and **Pen** to draw

Tip

Experiment with the pop-up menu to see what options are available.

Take note

You can Blackout your screen by pressing [B] or Whiteout your screen by pressing [W]. This could prove useful while you explain something, or show your audience something. Simply press [B] or [W] again to restore the Slide view.

(2) Drag the pointer to draw

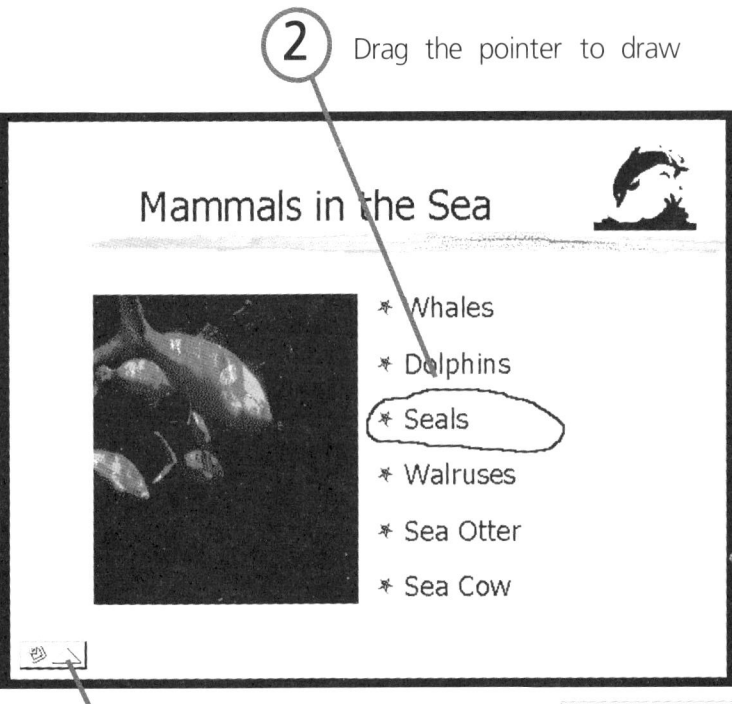

Mammals in the Sea

* Whales
* Dolphins
* (Seals)
* Walruses
* Sea Otter
* Sea Cow

Click to open the control panel

❑ **To 'draw' on the slides**

1 Press [Ctrl]-[P] to change the mouse pointer to a pen.

2 Click and drag to draw.

3 Press [Ctrl]-[A] to change the mouse pointer back to an arrow shape when you've finished.

❑ **To erase your drawing**

4 Press [E] on your keyboard.

Take note

To get more help on the options available while running a Slide Show, press [F1]. The Slide Show Help dialog box lists other options you might want to experiment with.

Slide Show Help ☒

During the slide show: [OK]

Left click, space, 'N', right or down arrow, enter, or page down	Advance to the next slide
Backspace, 'P', left or up arrow, or page up	Return to the previous slide
Number followed by Enter	Go to that slide
'B' or '.'	Blacks/Unblacks the screen
'W' or ','	Whites/Unwhites the screen
'A' or '='	Show/Hide the arrow pointer
'S' or '+'	Stop/Restart automatic show
Esc, Ctrl+Break, or '-'	End slide show
'E'	Erase drawing on screen
'H'	Go to hidden slide
'T'	Rehearse - Use new time
'O'	Rehearse - Use original time
'M'	Rehearse - Advance on mouse click
Hold both buttons down for 2 secs.	Return to first slide
Ctrl+P	Change pointer to pen
Ctrl+A	Change pointer to arrow
Ctrl+H	Hide pointer and button
Ctrl+L	Hide pointer and button always
Right mouse click	Popup menu/Previous slide

Basic steps

Summary Slide

1 Hold [Shift] and click to select the slides you wish to produce a Summary Slide from.

2 Click  the **Summary Slide** tool on the Slide Sorter toolbar.

You can get PowerPoint to automatically produce a Summary Slide for your presentation. The Summary Slide is placed in front of the other slides in your presentation. PowerPoint takes the title of each slide you select and lists it on the Summary Slide.

① Select the slides

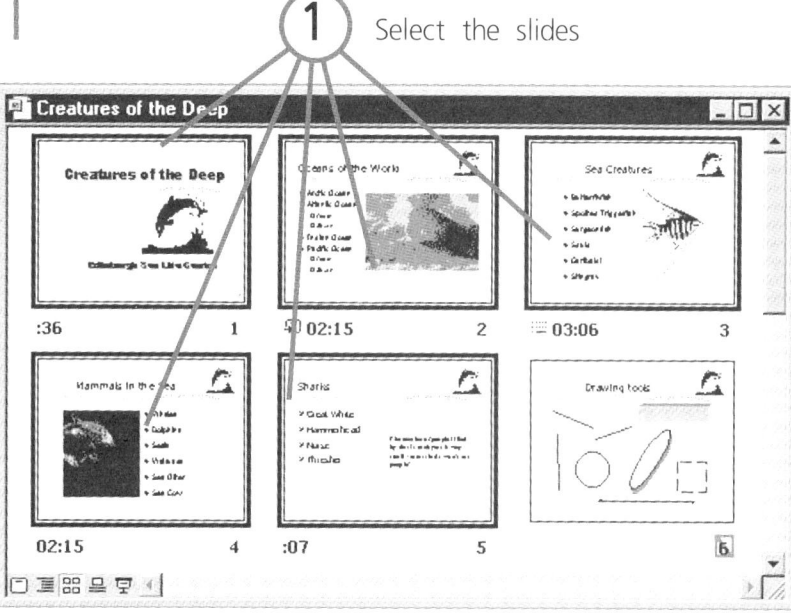

The Summary Slide will appear at the beginning

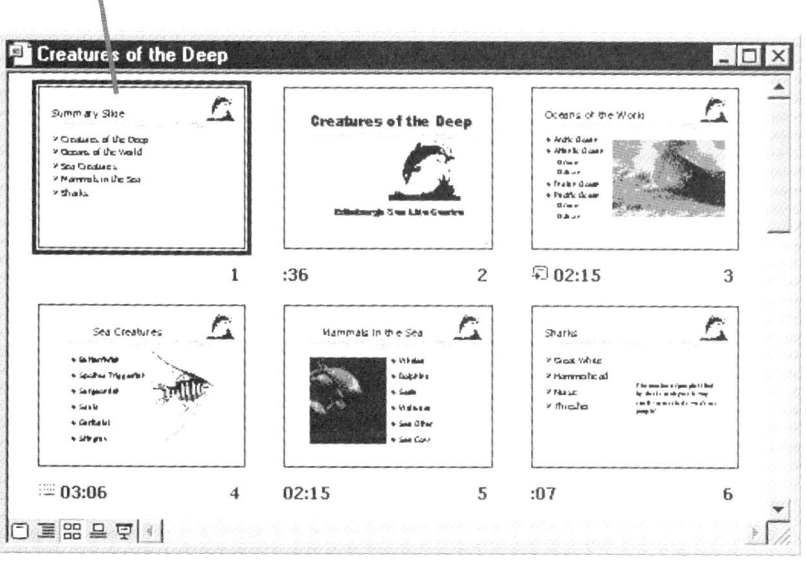

Summary

❑ SlideSorter view can be useful when **preparing a slide show** for presentation on your computer, as well as for moving your slides around.

❑ Slides that you may not need can be **Hidden**, but remain easily accessible should you require them during the presentation.

❑ **Transitions** are special effects that can be used to introduce a slide during a slide show. Use them to modify the way your slides advance during the presentation.

❑ Try the **Preset Animation** feature to gradually build up the main points on your slide.

❑ Practise your presentation with the **Rehearse Timings** facility to get your pace right.

❑ **Slide timings** can be set manually from the Transition dialog box or automatically using from Rehearse Timings.

❑ **Run your Slide Show** as you develop your presentation – it'll help you check how effective your choices are.

❑ The **pop-up menu** and **Slide Show Help** dialog box list the various options available to you when running your slide show.

❑ PowerPoint can create **Summary Slides** from the titles of your other slides.

11 Printing presentations

Slide format

You can print your whole presentation in PowerPoint - the slides, speaker's notes pages, audience handouts and the presentation outline.

You can print copies of your slides onto paper or onto overhead transparencies, or you can create slides using a desktop film recorder, or get a bureau to create the slides for you.

The first stage to printing your presentation is to set up the slide format.

1 Choose **Page Setup** from the **File** menu.

2 Select the size from the **Slides sized for** field.

3 Specify the orientation required for the **Slides**.

4 Specify the orientation required for the **Notes, handouts & outline.**

5 Click [OK].

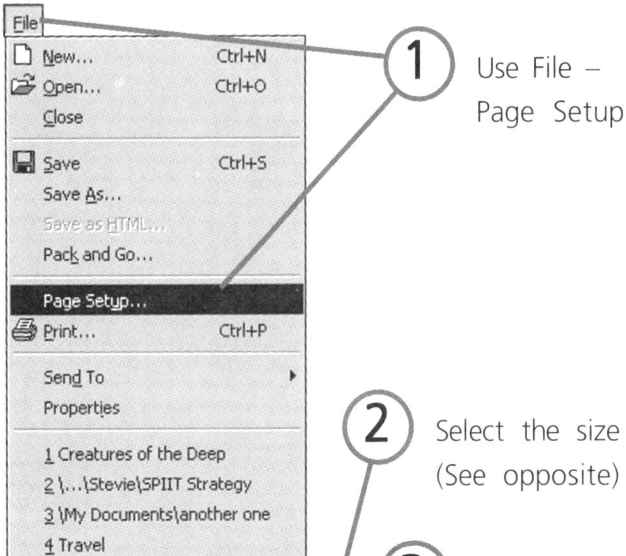

File menu:
- New...   Ctrl+N
- Open...   Ctrl+O
- Close
- Save   Ctrl+S
- Save As...
- Save as HTML...
- Pack and Go...
- Page Setup...
- Print...   Ctrl+P
- Send To   ▶
- Properties
- 1 Creatures of the Deep
- 2 \...\Stevie\SPIIT Strategy
- 3 \My Documents\another one
- 4 Travel
- Exit

(1) Use File – Page Setup

(2) Select the size (See opposite)

(3) Set the Slide Orientation

Take note

All slides in a presentation file must be in one orientation — either landscape or portrait.

To combine slides of different orientations in the same slide show, see Hyperlinks in the next chapter.

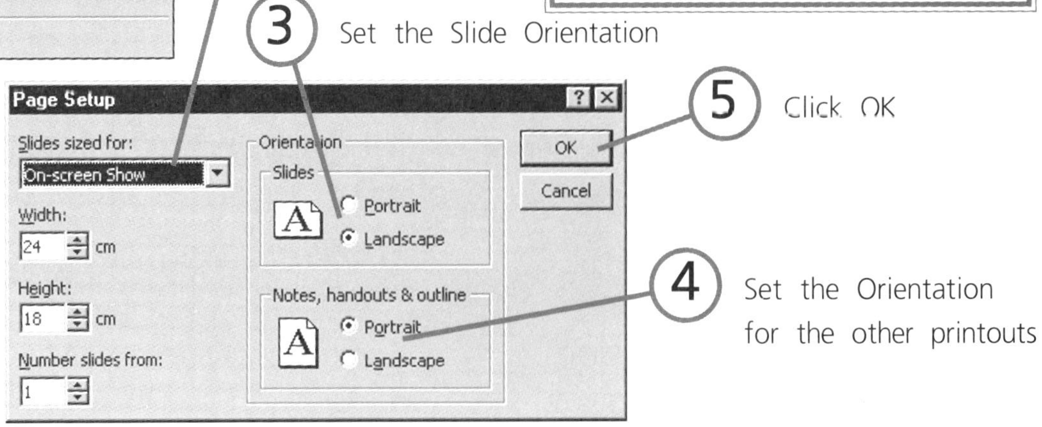

Page Setup

Slides sized for:
On-screen Show

Width: 24 cm

Height: 18 cm

Number slides from: 1

Orientation
- Slides: ○ Portrait ● Landscape
- Notes, handouts & outline: ● Portrait ○ Landscape

[OK] [Cancel]

(5) Click OK

(4) Set the Orientation for the other printouts

124

Slide sized for:

Type	Width	Height	Notes
On-screen show	24 cm	18 cm	Orientation to Landscape; 3:4 aspect ratio
Letter Paper	24 cm	18 cm	3:4 aspect ratio
A4 Paper	26 cm	18 cm	Aspect ratio between that of on-screen show and 35 mm slides
35mm Slides	27 cm	18 cm	Content will fill the slide in landscape orientation 2:3 aspect ratio
Overhead	24 cm	18 cm	Select for overhead transparencies
Banner	19.2 cm	2.4 cm	
Custom			Set own measurements required

Printing slides

With the Slide Setup details specified to give the output required, you can go ahead and print your slides.

1 Open the **File** menu and choose **Print**.

2 Specify the **Print range** to print.

3 Set the **Number of copies**, if required.

4 Select one of the **Slide** options from the **Print What**: list – see notes opposite.

5 Click [OK].

File

New...	Ctrl+N
Open...	Ctrl+O
Close	
Save	Ctrl+S
Save As...	
Save as HTML...	
Pack and Go...	
Page Setup...	
Print...	Ctrl+P
Send To	▶
Properties	
1 Creatures of the Deep	
2 \...\Stevie\SPIIT Strategy	
3 \My Documents\another one	
4 Travel	
Exit	

Select File – Print

Set the range

How many copies?

Set the Slide option

Print - Creatures of the Deep

Printer

Name: Star LC24-10 [Properties]

Status: Idle
Type: Star LC24-10
Where: LPT1:
Comment:

☐ Print to file

Print range

○ All
○ Current slide   ○ Selection
○ Custom Show:
○ Slides:

Enter slide numbers and/or slide ranges. For example, 1,3,5-12

Copies

Number of copies: [1]

☑ Collate

Print what: Slides (without animations)

☑ Print hidden slides

☑ Black & white   ☐ Scale to fit paper
☐ Pure black & white   ☐ Frame slides

[OK]   [Cancel]

Click OK

126

Print what: options

Slides

Prints your slides on paper or overhead transparencies, one slide per page. This option is only available when there are no slides with text animation in your presentation.

Slides (with animations)

Prints each step of an animated slide, one image per page, starting with the Slide Title, then each major bullet item in the text.

Slides (without animations)

Prints one page per slide, with all items included on it.

Take note

If you are going to send your slides to a service bureau to be turned into 35 mm slides or other materials, choose the Print to File option in the Print dialog box. It is important that you know what printer will print your file - select the appropriate printer name from the Name field. PowerPoint will display the Save As dialog box (so you can give your file a name) when you click OK.

For additional information read the on-line Help or contact the bureau you will be sending the files to.

Printing notes pages

It is useful to print out your notes pages to help ensure you cover all the relevant points during your presentation. When these are printed, a copy of the slide is placed at the top of the page and your notes appear below it.

Basic steps

1 Choose **Print** from the **File** menu.

2 Select **Notes Page** from **Print what**.

3 Set the **Print range**.

4 Click [OK].

③ Set the range

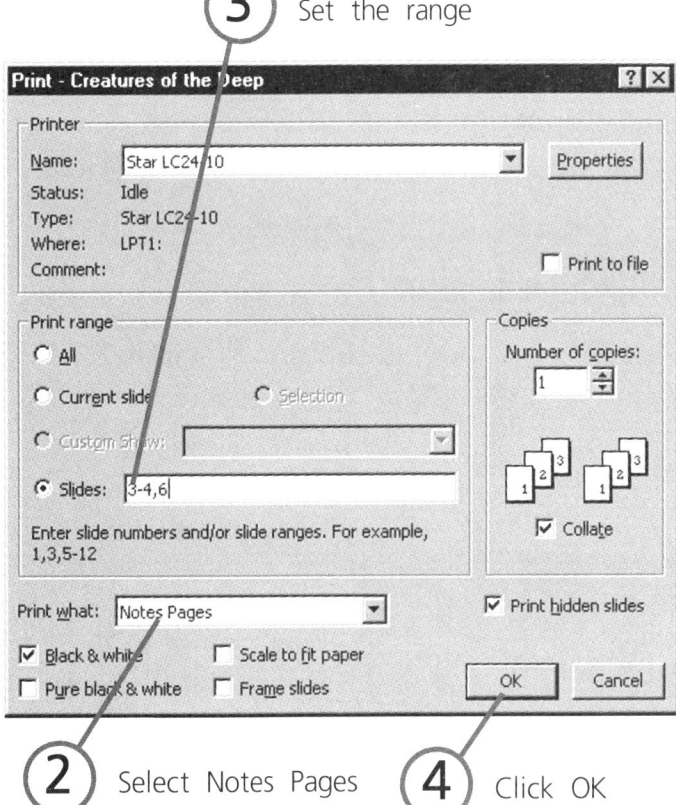

② Select Notes Pages

④ Click OK

Take note

Page numbers are added automatically, unless you removed the number field from the Notes Master.

Take note

If you click the Print icon on the standard toolbar, one copy of each slide is printed. For anything else you must access the Print dialog box and select what you want to print in the Print what: field.

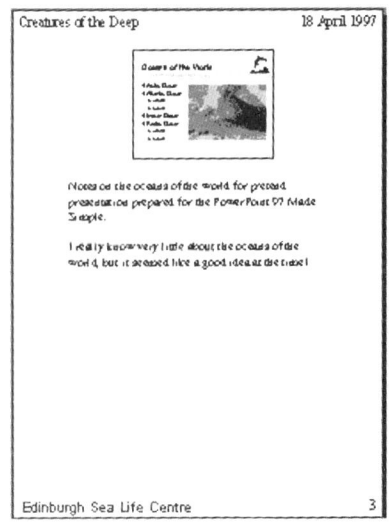

Basic steps

1 Choose **Print** from the **File** menu.

2 Select **Handouts** (2 slides, 3 slides or 6 slides per page as required).

3 Set the **Print range**.

4 Click [OK].

You can print copies of your slides out to issue as audience handouts. The format of the handout can be set up to include 2, 3 or 6 slides to the page.

If you want to add text, Clip art, etc. to your handouts, you must edit the Handouts Master page.

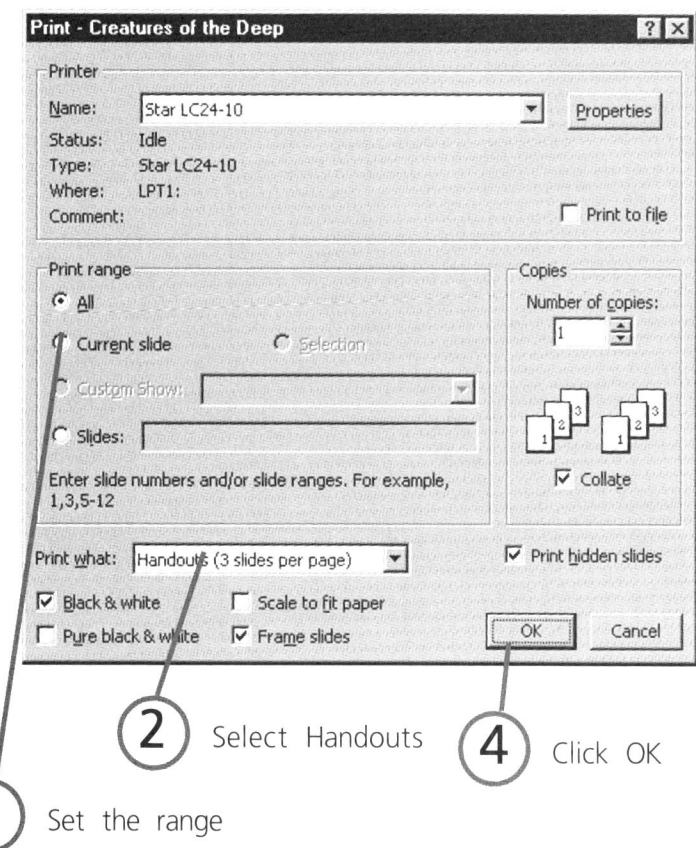

③ Set the range

② Select Handouts

④ Click OK

Tip

The 6 slides per page option is a good way to get a summary for your own use. The 3 slides per page option is probably better for your audience as it includes lines down the right side of the page for them to make their own notes.

See examples on next page.

Take note

You can print Hidden slides on your handouts, even if you skip them during the presentation.

Handout printed 3 slides to a page

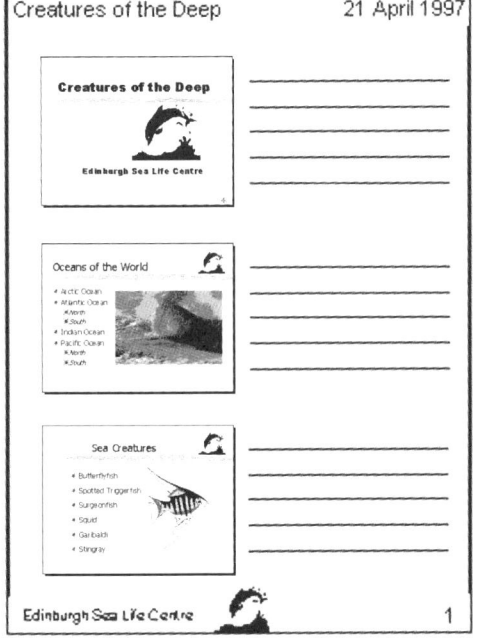

Handout printed 2 slides to a page

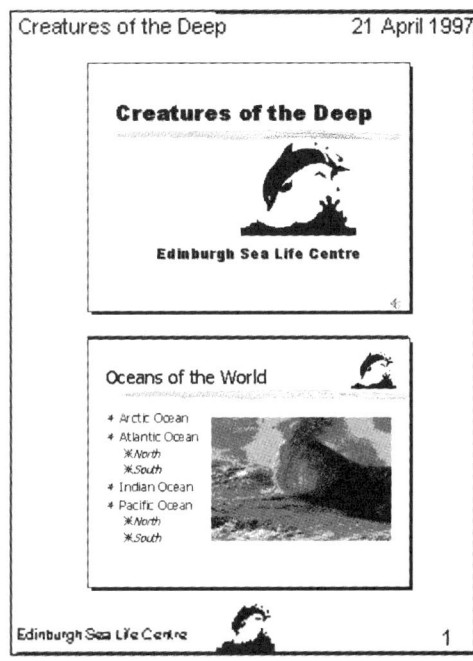

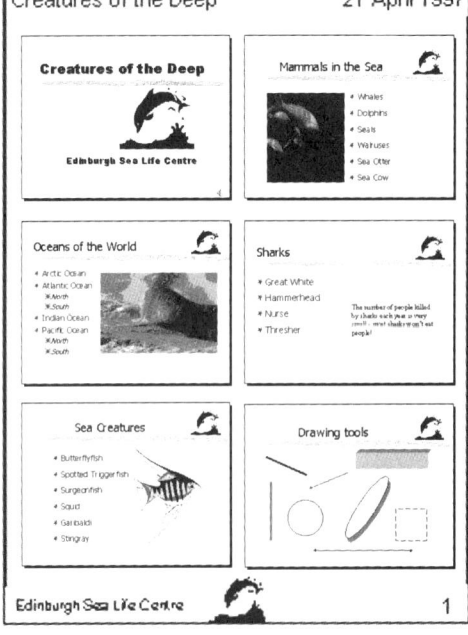

Handout printed
6 slides to a page

Basic steps

1 Choose **Print** from the **File** menu.

2 Select **Outline View**.

3 Specify the **Print range**.

4 Click [OK].

If you wish to print out a copy of the Outline view of your presentation, the same basic techniques are used. Your print will contain details of each slide title and the main points listed on each slide.

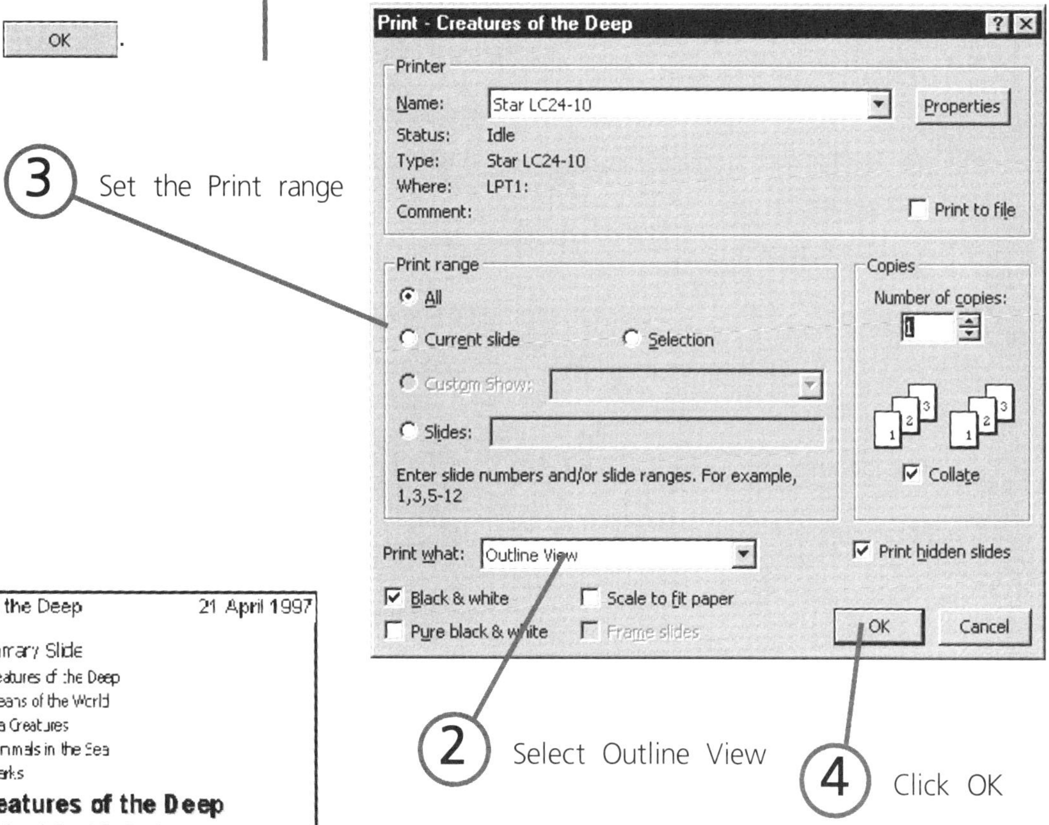

③ Set the Print range

Print - Creatures of the Deep [?][X]

Printer

Name: Star LC24-10 [▼] [Properties]
Status: Idle
Type: Star LC24-10
Where: LPT1:
Comment: [ ] Print to file

Print range
- (•) All
- ( ) Current slide   ( ) Selection
- ( ) Custom Show: [_____▼]
- ( ) Slides: [_____]

Enter slide numbers and/or slide ranges. For example, 1,3,5-12

Copies
Number of copies: [1] [▲▼]
[✓] Collate

Print what: [Outline View ▼]
[✓] Black & white   [ ] Scale to fit paper
[ ] Pure black & white [ ] Frame slides

[✓] Print hidden slides

[OK] [Cancel]

② Select Outline View

④ Click OK

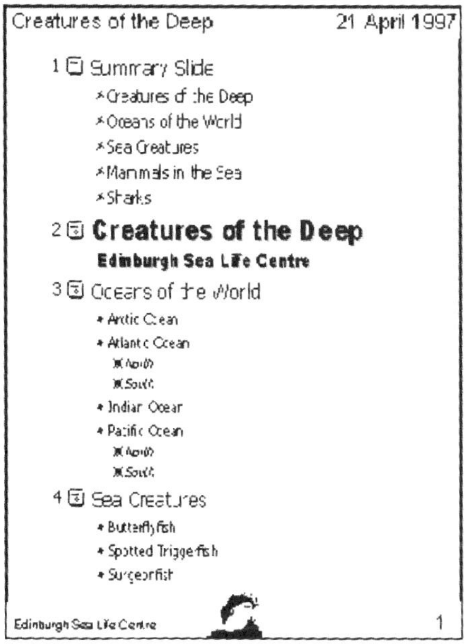

Creatures of the Deep   21 April 1997

1 ▣ Summary Slide
   * Creatures of the Deep
   * Oceans of the World
   * Sea Creatures
   * Mammals in the Sea
   * Sharks
2 ▣ **Creatures of the Deep**
   Edinburgh Sea Life Centre
3 ▣ Oceans of the World
   • Arctic Ocean
   • Atlantic Ocean
      ✗ North
      ✗ South
   • Indian Ocean
   • Pacific Ocean
      ✗ North
      ✗ South
4 ▣ Sea Creatures
   • Butterflyfish
   • Spotted Triggerfish
   • Surgeonfish

Edinburgh Sea Life Centre   1

Tip

A printed Outline can be very useful in that it lets you see an overview of the whole presentation.

Summary

❏ Specify your **slide format** before printing your presentation.

❏ You can choose to print your slides with or without **animation.**

❏ It is often easier to specify your **print range** (if you don't want to print all of your slides) in Slide Sorter view.

❏ Print the **Notes page** to act as prompts while you give your presentation.

❏ **Handouts** for your audiences can be printed with 2, 3 or 6 slides per page.

❏ Take a print of **Outline view** if you want a summary of your complete presentation.

12 Jumping and linking

Action Buttons

Action Buttons are found in the AutoShapes list on the Drawing toolbar. You can use the Action Buttons to jump from one place in your presentation to another, or to link you through to another presentation, file or program.

The Action Buttons can be added to any slide you wish – they become 'activated' when you are running your slide show on a computer.

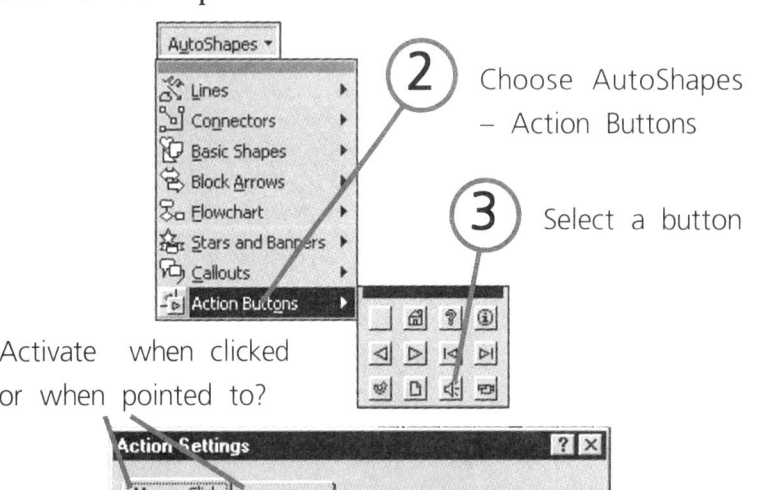

Choose AutoShapes – Action Buttons

Select a button

Activate when clicked or when pointed to?

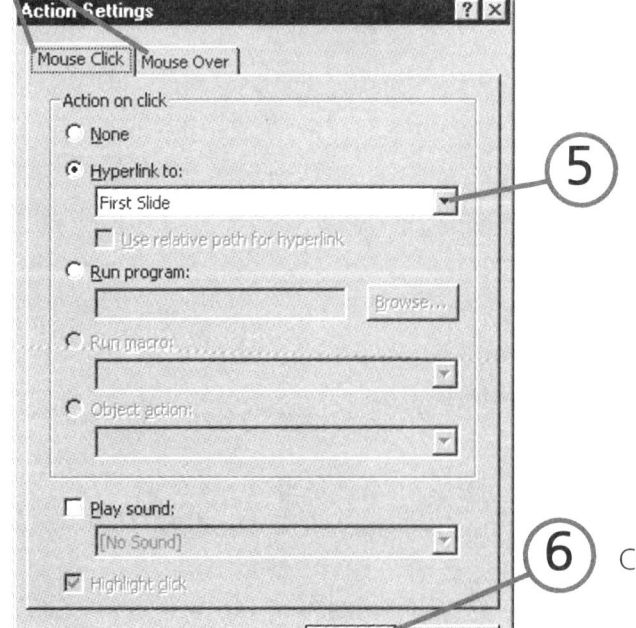

Link to a slide

Click OK

1 Display the slide you want to put an Action Button on.

2 Choose **Action Buttons** from the **AutoShapes** menu.

3 Select a button.

4 Click on your slide to indicate where you want the button to appear.

5 At the **Action Settings** dialog box, select the slide to **Hyperlink to**.

6 Click [OK].

7 Resize or reposition the Action Button if necessary.

> **Tip**
>
> I suggest you go to Slide view for this section.

134

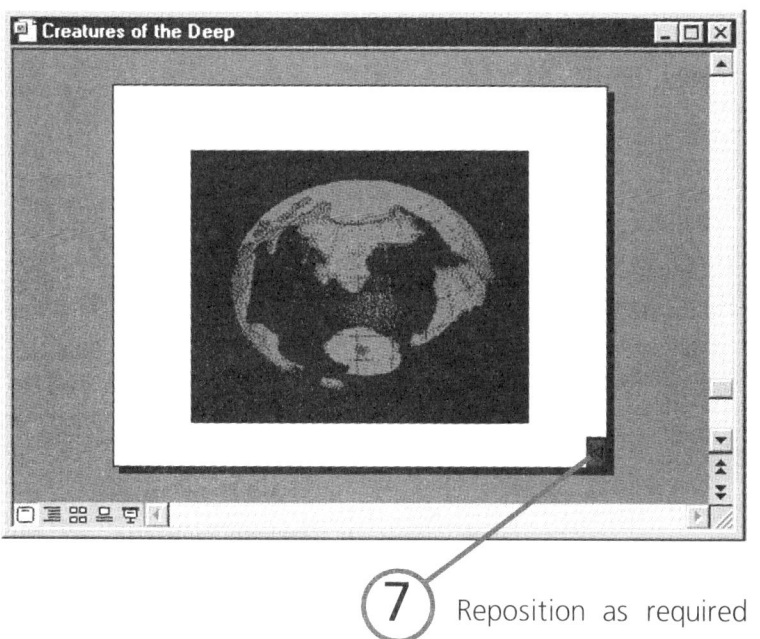

⑦ Reposition as required

Take note

Most of the Action Buttons have default settings – you can change these in the Action Settings dialog box.

To edit the settings of an existing Button, right click on the button and choose Action Settings from the short cut menu.

Tip

If you like adding Action Buttons to your slides, make the Action Buttons submenu a floating menu (drag its title bar) – to give you quick access to all the buttons. You can 'dock' the menu at the top, bottom, right or left of your screen.

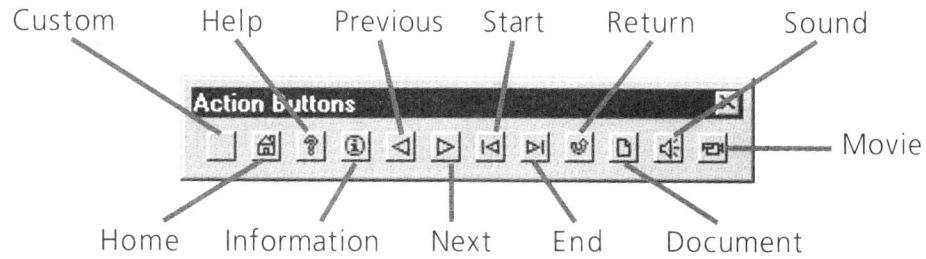

Custom   Help   Previous   Start   Return   Sound

Movie

Home   Information   Next   End   Document

Sound and movies

We have already added sounds and movies to our slides using the Insert Object command (see Chapter 8). You can also use Action Buttons to activate sounds or movies in your presentation.

- You'll find sounds on the Office 97 CD, in the folders:

  Office97/Office97pro/ClipArt/Mmedia
  Office97/Office97pro/ Sounds

- For movies, look in the folder:

  Office97/Office97pro/ClipArt/Mmedia

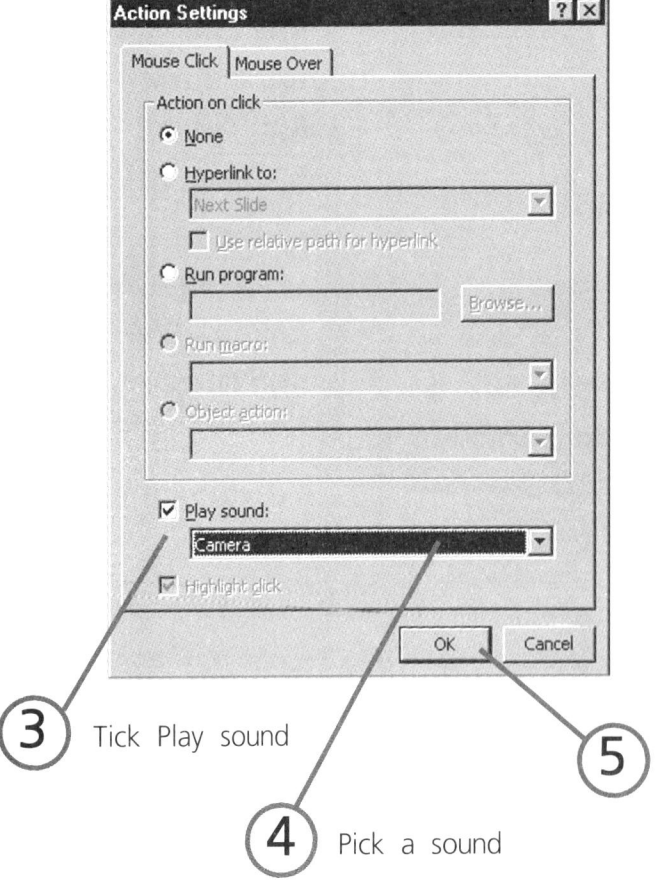

③ Tick Play sound

④ Pick a sound

⑤ Click OK

1 Choose the Action Button – Sound 📢 or Movie 📹.

2 Click on your slide to position the button.

❑ **Sounds**

3 Select the **Play sound** checkbox.

4 Choose a sound from the list, or choose **Other Sound...** and locate the sound file required.

5 Click [OK].

❑ **Movies**

6 Select **Hyperlink to:**

7 Choose **Other File** from the list.

8 Locate your chosen movie file.

Actions can happen when you click the mouse, or pass the mouse over the button

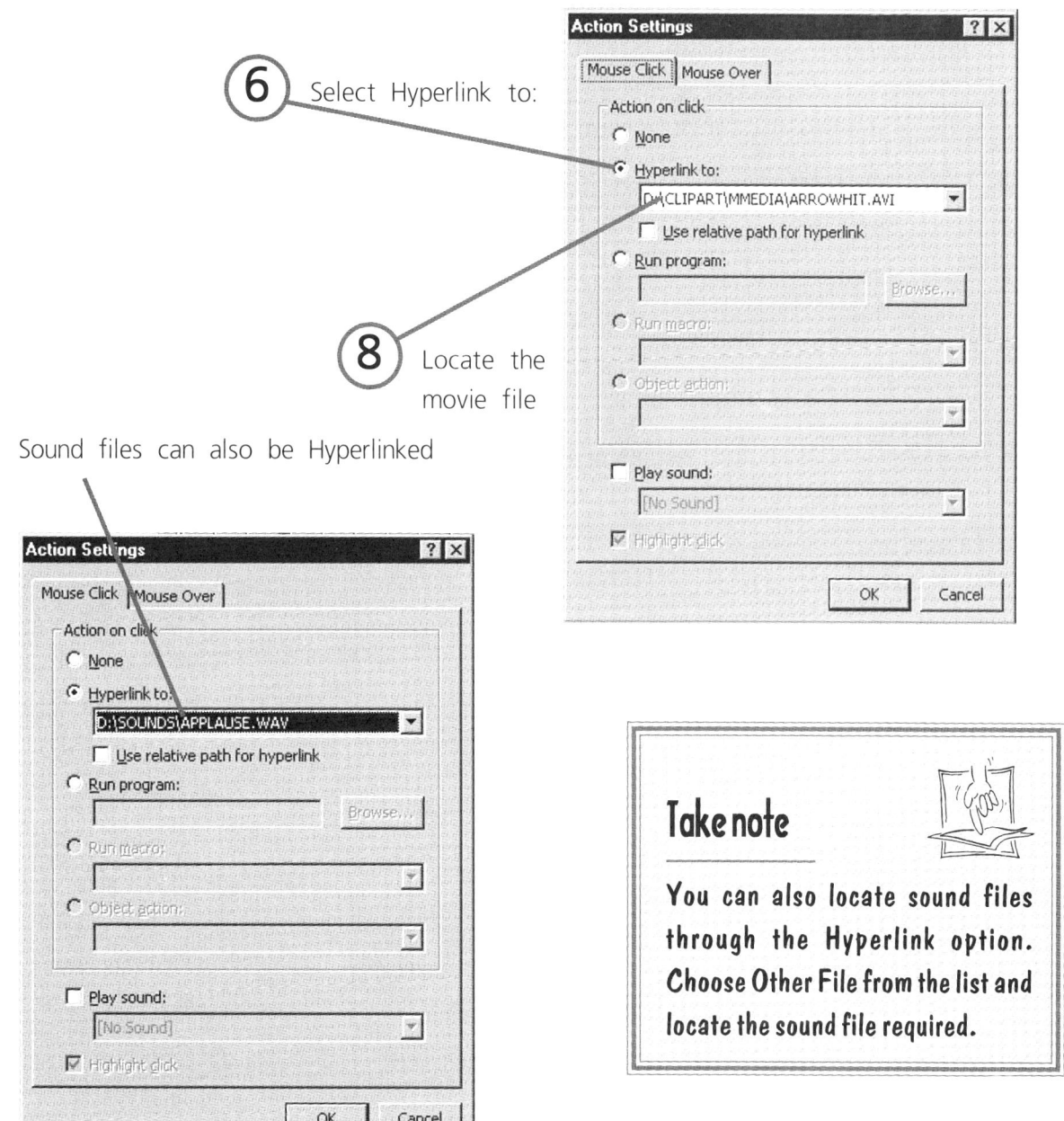

⑥ Select Hyperlink to:

⑧ Locate the movie file

Sound files can also be Hyperlinked

Take note

You can also locate sound files through the Hyperlink option. Choose Other File from the list and locate the sound file required.

Mixed slide orientation

In any PowerPoint file, the slide orientation is either landscape (the default) or portrait. You can't have some of the slides landscape and some portrait in the same file. If you want a presentation with some in one orientation and some in the other, Action Buttons and Hyperlinks can help out. You need to set up two files – one with the slide orientation landscape and the other portrait.

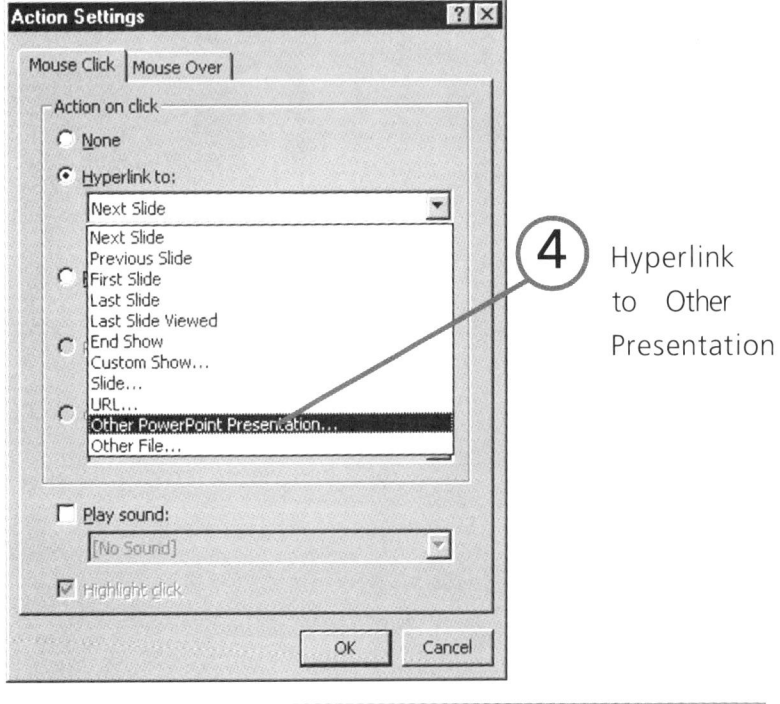

Hyperlink to Other Presentation

Take note

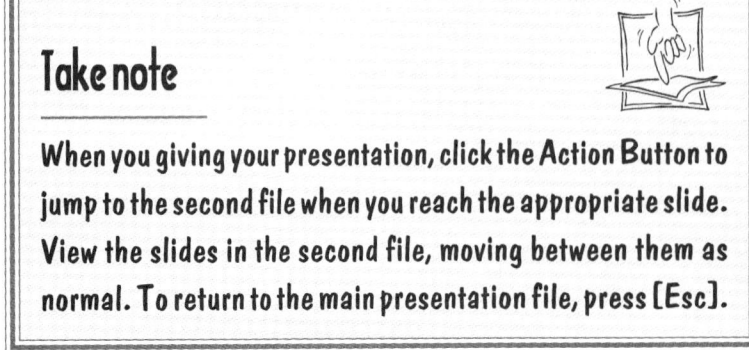

When you giving your presentation, click the Action Button to jump to the second file when you reach the appropriate slide. View the slides in the second file, moving between them as normal. To return to the main presentation file, press [Esc].

Basic steps

1 Set up your main presentation file – leaving out any slides that are in the other orientation.

2 Set up a second file with the remaining slides – with the other slide orientation set.

3 In the main presentation file, place an Action Button on the slide that precedes a slide from the second file – I suggest you use the Custom button.

4 In **Hyperlink to:** choose **Other PowerPoint Presentation.**

5 Select the file that contains your slide(s) and click [OK].

6 Specify the slide you want to jump to.

7 Click [OK] to close the **Hyperlink to Slide** dialog box.

8 Click [OK] to close the **Action Settings** dialog box.

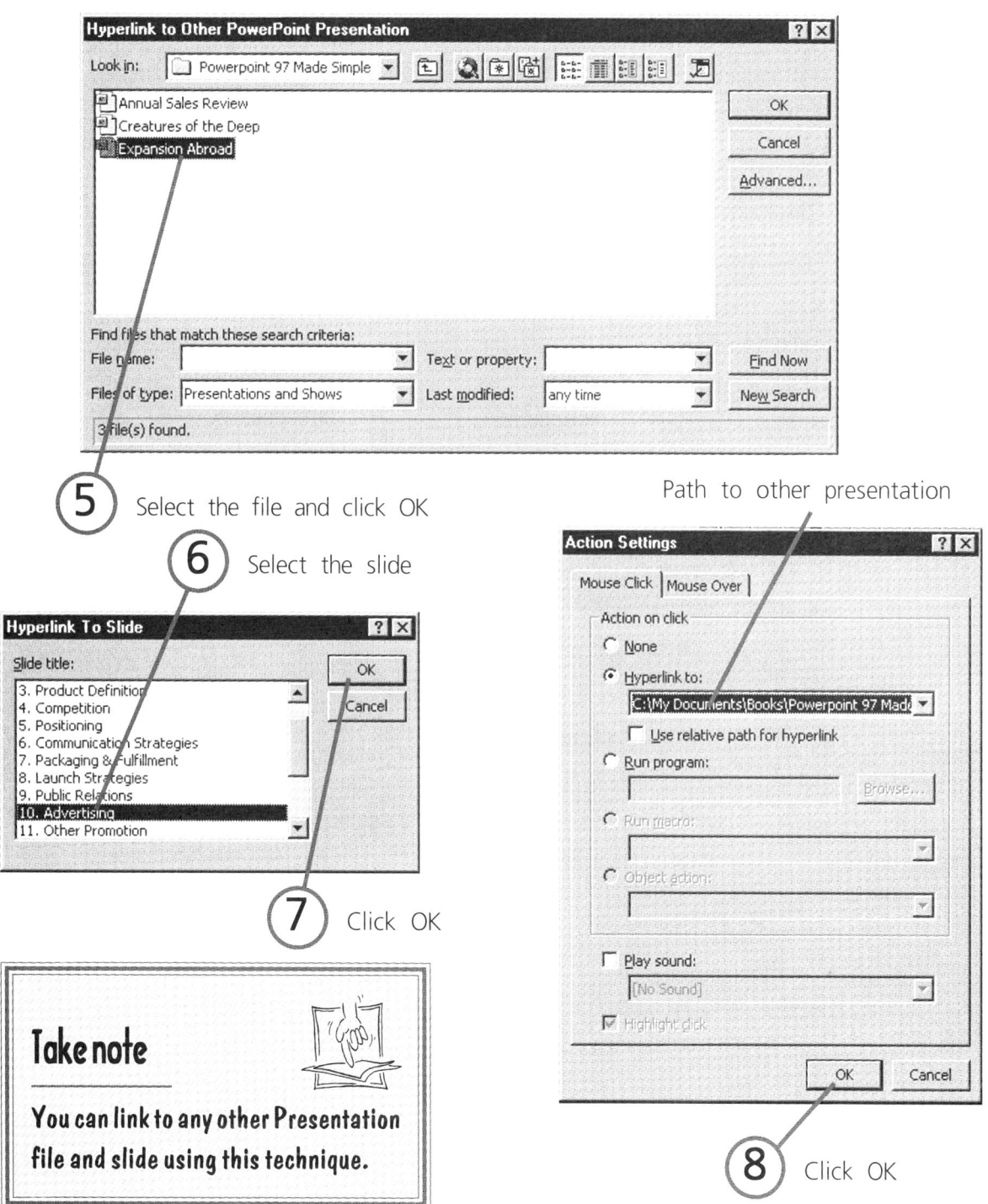

Select the file and click OK

Select the slide

Path to other presentation

Click OK

Click OK

Take note

You can link to any other Presentation file and slide using this technique.

Hyperlink from any object

You don't have to use Action Buttons to hyperlink to different places in your file, to another file or to an Internet address. You can attach a Hyperlink to most objects – Text, AutoShape, Clip art, WordArt, etc.

Basic steps

1 Select the object to hold the Hyperlink.

Or

Place the insertion point within the word to hold the Hyperlink.

2 Click  the **Insert Hyperlink** tool.

3 Type the path or Browse for the file you want to link – it could be on your disk, on your company Intranet or on the Internet.

4 Click ⬚ OK ⬚ .

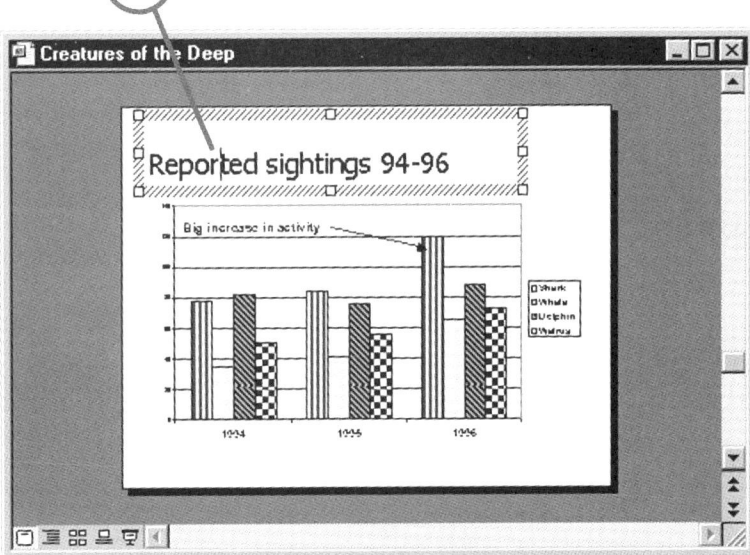

Select the word or object

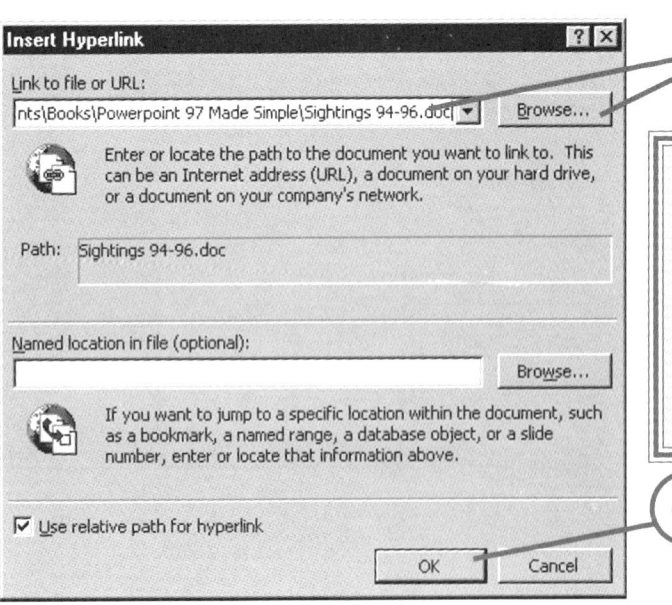

Type or browse for the path to the file

Click OK

Take note

When you jump to a Hyperlink document, click ⬅ **Back on the Web** toolbar to return to your presentation.

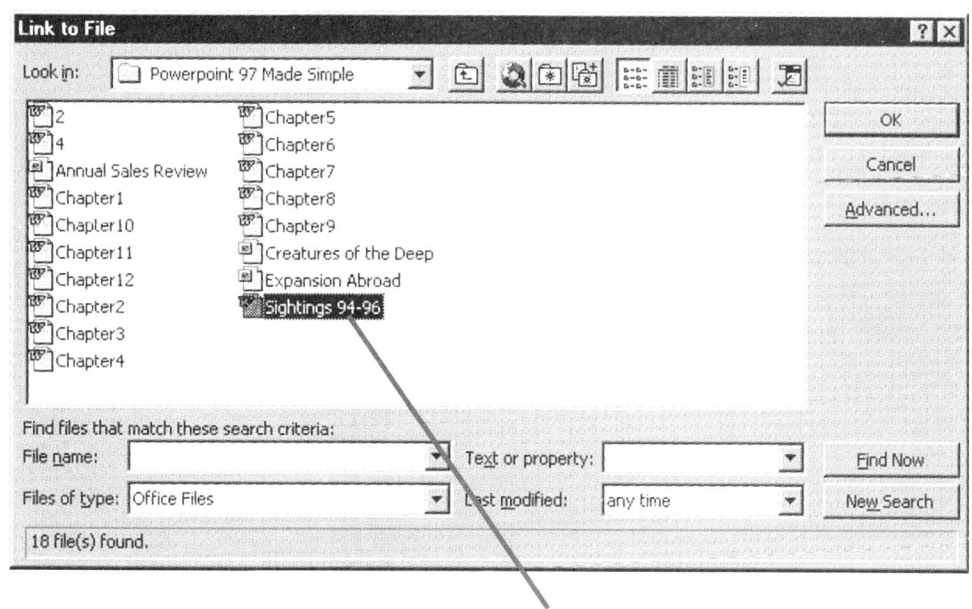

Look through your folders to find the file

Take note

During your slide show, you can 'jump' to the Hyperlink using your chosen method – either 'mouse click' or 'mouse over'.

Hyperlinked words are displayed with underlining and in a different colour

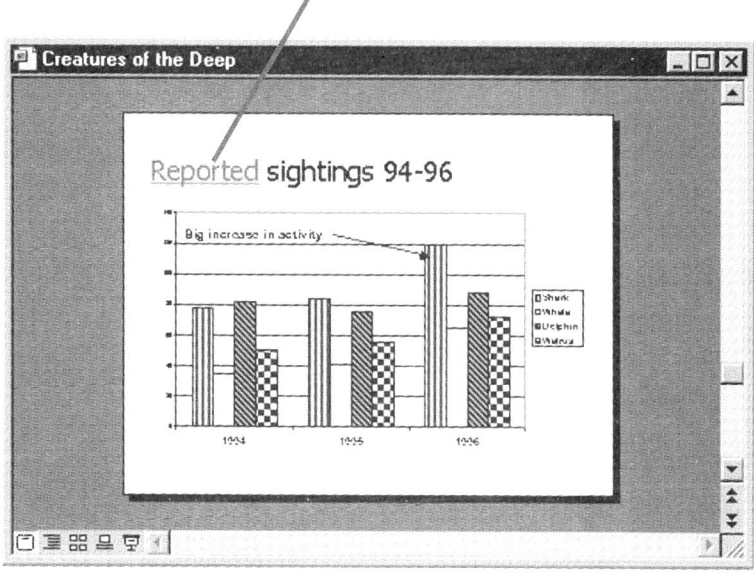

Summary

❏ **Action Buttons** provide a quick point and click method of **jumping** between slides, files and Internet addresses.

❏ **Sounds** and **movies** can be attached to Action Buttons.

❏ If you have **different slide orientations** within one presentation, create two separate files (one for each orientation) and insert Hyperlinks between the two files as necessary.

❏ **Hyperlinks** can be attached to most of the object types on your slides.

Index